LINE OF PAIN

(WAR TO PEACE)

BASED ON A TRUE STORY

ROZINA KHANAM

BlueRose ONE.com
Stories Matter
NewDelhi • London

BLUEROSE PUBLISHERS
India | U.K.

For permissions, requests or inquiries regarding this publication, please contact:

BLUEROSE PUBLISHERS
www.BlueRoseONE.com
info@bluerosepublishers.com
+91 8882 898 898
+4407342408967

ISBN: 978-93-7139-102-3

Cover Design: Shubham Verma
Typesetting: Sagar

First Edition: July 2025

DISCLAIMER

This story is based on the author's personal experiences. Any resemblance to any persons, incidents, or situations is purely coincidental. The author assumes no responsibility for any resemblance or similarity

DEDICATION

I dedicate this book to my parents and to all those who have travelled on the path of thorns, suffered, and shared this pain equally. This book is a tribute to all those Men, Women, and Children martyred in India, Pakistan, and Bangladesh (sub-continent) since the partition of the subcontinent who have been killed innocently in the war of colour, race, and religion.

Rozina Khanam

ACKNOWLEDGEMENT

After a few years of marriage, my father, Shamim Ahmad Khan, left Patna in search of employment and a better future and moved to Dhaka. Later, my mother also joined him there. It was from Dhaka that a new chapter of my life began.

This is the story of my parents and my life. A tale written in tears in some places, and wiped by tears in others.

My early education took place in Dhaka. After that, I studied for almost two years in Meerut, an Indian city, during a period of being a war prisoner.

Later, I continued my education in Karachi, Pakistan, from Grade 4 to matriculation at Happy Home English School. I completed my B. Com from Government Premier College in Karachi, which is affiliated with the University of Karachi.

My father wanted me to become a Chartered Accountant, but due to the worsening situation in Karachi at the time, I couldn't continue my education despite getting admission. By then, the Muhajir Qaumi Movement had been established. Since Karachi University was near my home, I gave up the idea of CA and got admission in MA English. However, before the results were announced, I got married on July 16, 1990, and moved to India.

After coming to India, the first difficulty I faced was that I couldn't work anywhere because until I obtained Indian citizenship, my certificates were of no use. It was a major concern for me that I couldn't make proper use of my education.

Since childhood, I had seen my parents helping people even in the worst situations, so this quality was in my blood. My grandfather and uncle were also quite socially active.

When I became restless from sitting idle, my friend Saroj Choubey said, you can at least do social work. Why don't you join an NGO? At that time, I didn't even know what an NGO was, but my passion for social work gave me the courage, and I gathered the strength to move forward.

In the year 2000, I began my journey in social work, and my very first project was with UNICEF, in which I conducted several polio awareness programs with school children. Mr. Augustine from UNICEF encouraged me greatly and helped me understand NGO work and progress in it. After that, I never looked back it felt like I had found my true calling.

Seeing my passion, my husband, Arshad Khan, founded the Women Welfare Society of Patna in the year 2000 itself, in which I got the opportunity to work as the Project Director. Gradually, Rozina Khanam became the identity of the Women Welfare Society of Patna not just its identity, but also the voice of Muslim women.

On March 7, 2006, I received an invitation from Abu Saleh Shariff (Member Secretary, High-Level Committee) to attend a round-table meeting that was to be held under the supervision of Chairman Justice Rajinder Sachar in Delhi on April 10, 2006. I was to present a report on the backwardness of Muslim women in Bihar, which focused on their social, economic, and educational disadvantages.

This was the first major achievement of my social work that I became a part of this report.

Seeing my work for Muslim women, the U.S. State Department selected me for their IVLP program (International Visitors Leadership Program) and invited me to visit the United States, where a global NGO meet was being held. The entire month of March 2008 had been declared Women's Month, and I was fortunate to be part of the program titled "The Role of Promotion of Global Women's Issues" from 6th March to 27th March 2008. During this time, I represented India across seven U.S. states.

On the other hand, I was also raising my voice for Muslim women regarding the Women's Reservation Bill, and in this regard, I had been sending letters to both the Rajya Sabha and the Lok Sabha. On 6th July 2009, I received a letter from the Lok Sabha Secretariat inviting me to appear before the Standing Committee to represent the voices of Muslim women and speak about their need for reservation.

In July 2008, Patna Airport appointed me as a member of the Anti-Sexual Harassment Committee for Employees for 2008–2009, and again for 2009 –2010. I continued as a member there until 2010–2011. After that, I joined the same committee at the Zonal Office of the Central Bank of India, where I served from 2015–2016, 2016–2017, and 2017–2018. Later, due to some personal commitments, I eventually stepped down from all these roles.

These were a few of my major achievements, or one could say contributions, that I was able to contribute during my social work career.

In 2006, seeing my growing interest in social work, my husband, Arshad Khan, offered a part of our home to open a training centre for girls. There, I provided training in various skills such as sewing, embroidery, beautician courses, computer education, and other vocational programs.

I had my unique approach to social work; I decided that I would neither earn money from it nor take on large government projects.

However, I still needed to run the centre and support the girls. So, I came up with a solution: I started taking small awareness programs from UNICEF, ICDS, and the Government Health Department. The income generated from these programs was spent entirely on the girls' welfare.

During this time, I observed that most of the girls coming to my centre relied on sewing as their primary means of livelihood, as they were not well-educated.

I approached Bharat Petroleum, suggesting that if they could support these girls, it would greatly help improve their financial condition. Accepting my proposal, Bharat Petroleum generously donated 200 sewing machines to my girls, which proved to be of great use in building their futures.

While training these girls, I realized that it would be beneficial to also encourage them toward formal education. Furthermore, having a government-certified vocational training certificate would enhance their opportunities.

Though my NGO was already issuing certificates, they were not sufficient. After much effort and follow-up, I successfully affiliated with NIOS for vocational training, NCPUL for Urdu promotional programs, and NILLET for certified computer courses.

By 2015, I had provided over 5,000 girls with vocational and computer training along with government-recognized certification through my centre.

However, due to some personal challenges and responsibilities that arose in the same year, I had to shift my focus to my family. I shifted to Delhi for four years, which limited my time and engagement in social work.

With the arrival of COVID-19 and because I was still in Delhi, I was forced to close down my centre, something that remains a source of deep regret for me.

Today, my social work is limited to online counselling, but I am truly happy that those girls I trained are now living successful and independent lives.

I would like to acknowledge here that in the journey and struggles of life, my husband, Arshad Khan, truly fulfilled the role of a life partner. He was not only with me in times of joy and sorrow, but also encouraged me at every step. He provided immense support in the writing and publication of this book as well.

A BRIEF LOOK

Since the beginning of time, stories and tales have been written across every corner of the world sometimes about love, sometimes about hatred, sometimes about humanity, and at other times about politics. But the one thing that has caused the most pain to mankind throughout history is politics.

In every part of the world, politics has wreaked havoc. Innocent people are being killed, and countless are being displaced from their homes. Politics itself is not evil, but treating human beings as mere tools for the sake of power is fundamentally wrong.

What has negative politics given the world? Racism in some places, religious division in others, casteism somewhere else, nationalism elsewhere and hatred in the name of identity. The struggle for power and dominance has engulfed the entire world.

As a result, thousands have become homeless, countless women widowed, millions of children orphaned, and an unknown number of young girls have been dishonoured or murdered, who neither had any fault nor even understood why they were being killed.

The worth of a human being has been reduced to that of insects, there is often no one even willing to hear the cries of the oppressed.

Scenes like these are scattered across every region of the world, and one can always find stories of this nature. Similar stories continue to emerge from our land as well.

The struggle for power and the resulting devastation and ruin of the common people is a tale as old as the beginning of creation. Blood-soaked stories of political games and the thirst for power have existed from ancient India to modern India.

New chapters of this saga include the various phases of the freedom movement and the painful partition of independent India. From the womb of partition were born countless heartbreaking stories, drawing deep lines of sorrow and anguish. Writers and creative minds have brought these incidents and tales of pain and suffering before the world.

We have heard and seen countless stories related to India and Pakistan, and no matter what the creators' intention behind those films or narratives was, the viewers and listeners have, to this day, failed to grasp the message they were trying to convey.

Our generations either never learned any real lessons from them, or the lessons they took were shaped by their mindset, a mindset formed by deliberate conditioning.

The lasting impression that settled in people's minds is one of hatred. Hatred towards those who were once our own. In these stories, every individual sees one community oppressing another. Some narratives depict religious conflicts; others sow the seeds of hatred. Rarely does anyone try to understand the message of humanity. People often take away the Two-Nation Theory, which is precisely why we are failing to offer anything meaningful to our future generations.

If we are passing something down, it is the battle of colour, religion, and caste. In today's age, the spirit of freedom, patriotism, and sacrifice has been buried deep. Brotherhood, love, and humanity have all been consumed by the ideology of division.

Today, I bring forth a true story from that very past; a story that teaches the lesson of humanity. It is a tale of those whose own homeland turned into a prison, where they became war prisoners (POWs) mere puppets in the hands of a handful of political figures. These people are still wandering; in search of a livelihood and a place they can call their own.

This is the story of those unfortunate souls who became victims of the Two-Nation Theory. It is a story of war and of the people caught within it that carries a message of peace, love, and brotherhood, but only if one is willing to understand it in the right context.

This is not just the story of a single family; it is the story of all those who were forced to leave behind their homes and homelands and became muhajirs (refugees).

It is the story of martyrs who were never truly at fault, and yet, to this day, their descendants, their families, continue to bear the punishment.

The Indian subcontinent, a land where thousands came and ruled for centuries, from Gautam Buddha to the Mughals and later the British, has always been a cradle of diverse civilizations, cultures, races, and generosity. But when the

British arrived, the seeds of division based on colour, religion, and ethnicity began to take root.

Their strategy was simple yet effective: if you want to rule a nation, divide it along the lines of caste, creed, and ethnicity. And that's exactly what happened. The people of the subcontinent, who had lived together for centuries, slowly began to divide by caste, by community, and by religion.

Initially, they united to fight for freedom from British rule, but soon, internal divisions took deeper root. The idea of partition began to take shape, and eventually, it became a reality.

Before leaving, the British not only gifted the region the painful legacy of the Two-Nation Theory, but also, in the final act of partition, they left a dagger in our back in the form of Kashmir.

People who once lived like brothers now felt they could no longer co-exist, and thus emerged two new nations: India and Pakistan. But the divisions did not end there.

Not long after, a second partition took place, and Bangladesh was born and with it, many more stories of pain, betrayal, and displacement began to unfold on this blood-soaked land.

Drawing a line on the land does not divide relationships. That is why, when Partition happened, everything fell apart. Someone's heart was left on this side, their soul on the other. A son remained here, while a daughter was left behind there.

And so began a journey people leaving their land, abandoning their homes in search of a new dawn. From this side, they set out for Pakistan, and from the other side, they departed for India. The soil of the subcontinent drank the tears of blood in silence. From the depths of the earth, a sigh escaped, as if she were saying:

Nayi Manzil, Nayi Duniya, Nayi Zameen Par Jaane Walon
Tere Saath Isi Mitti ki Yaadein Aur Baatein Hongi
Samaet ke Le Jao Rang, Nasal aur Zaat-Paat Bhi
Agle Batwaare Mein Phir Inki Zarurat Hogi

To those who journey to new destinations, new worlds, new lands
You will carry the memories and stories of this very soil
Take with you your colours, your race, your caste as well
For in the next partition, they will be needed again

The people who migrated from various cities of India. whether from Uttar Pradesh, Bihar, or Bengal, mostly journeyed to East Pakistan (now Bangladesh), while some settled in Lahore and Karachi.

With dreams of a better future, these individuals set foot on the soil of East Pakistan, unaware that misfortune had not yet abandoned them, and that they were destined to witness yet another partition. And so, it happened once again, they were confronted with the Two-Nation Theory.

The remarkable thing this time was that the foundation of the Two-Nation Theory was not religion. This time, the reason was culture, heritage, and language and "language" itself became the basis for the new divide.

The small group of people who stepped onto the land of East Pakistan (now Bangladesh) were soon labelled as "outsiders," and voices began to rise from all directions shouting, "Amaar Sonar Desh" (My Golden Land) and demanding the expulsion of these outsiders. It was evident that this reaction stemmed from the politics of those in power in West Pakistan. Yet, the ones who truly suffered were these very migrants.

Even though, once again, these people were not at fault, they had left their homeland in search of better prospects and a brighter future, they still ended up paying the price. Their mistake, if any, was trusting that this new land would welcome them.

The conflict, in reality, was rooted in the political ambitions of West and East Pakistan, but the game was played using the tools of language and ethnicity. And in that game of politics, the innocent and simple-minded people were the ones caught in the crossfire.

This political tug-of-war escalated into extreme forms, spilling into violence and eventually into a full-fledged war. The real victims of this war were those so-called "outsiders," who had already left behind their homes, their land, and their roots to embrace a new country one that was never truly theirs to begin with.

The people who had migrated from various cities of India found themselves belonging neither here nor there. Once again, the cries for freedom and partition reverberated through the air, and soon a civil war erupted. Barely a few years had passed since the creation of Pakistan when yet another partition unfolded.

And once again, blood was shed. The Two-Nation Theory triumphed once more, but it was humanity that suffered the ultimate defeat.

Now these so-called "outsiders" became prisoners of war, and look at the irony of fate, where did they become prisoners? On the very soil of India, the land they had once left behind. It felt as though God above was laughing at mankind's foolishness, and the earth was whispering, Didn't I tell you not to leave me?

The world knows that 96,000 Pakistani soldiers were taken as prisoners of war during the Bangladesh War but very few are aware that among them were 32,000 civilians, who also became POWs. These prisoners were held across various cities in India, one of which was Meerut.

This is the story of those families who became prisoners of war in Meerut, families who lived every moment with the same haunting thought "What will happen now?" A strange and painful time it was. One brother was a prisoner, the other a guard.

There was a time when Hindus, Muslims, Sikhs, and Christians lived together, sharing joys and sorrows alike.

But now, a new era had dawned an era where one brother had no country, no shelter, and was held captive, while the other stood as his keeper, bound by duty to defend his homeland.

And the earth, weeping tears of blood, whispered softly:

Aankhon ne bhi ik ajeeb manzar dekha hai
Bhai ke ghar mein bhai ko qaid dekha hai
Kabhi rehte the jo mil ke majaaiyon ki tarah
Aaj ik ko muhafiz to doosre ko qaid dekha hai

Even these eyes have seen a strange, sorrowful sight
A brother imprisoned within his own brother's house
Once they lived together like hands of the same body
Now one stands guard, the other locked in chains

In the war that lasted fifteen days, the lives of thousands were forever changed. Thousands of innocent people from both nations were killed. Thousands more were displaced. They may have gained freedom, but never from the grip of politicians. Bangladesh came into existence, but even today, both regions remain troubled. After all, blood never spills in vain.

On the other side, those who had left their homes and lands behind became prisoners of war. Fate had played a cruel game, and it didn't end their fate had another act to unfold. When these prisoners were finally freed and sent back to Pakistan, what did they find? Nothing. Because the game of identity of nationhood was still being played, and continues to this day.

They tried to make the land of Sindh their own, but the locals gave them a label: "Lutay Pitay Bihari" the plundered and scattered Biharis. Even though these so-called Biharis included people from UP, Bihar, and other parts of India, they were labelled as outsiders by Bangladeshis, and now as "Lutay Pitay Bihari" by Pakistanis.

As if that weren't enough, when their status rose a little, they were given another title: "Muhajir" the migrant. And so, they came to be known by this name. Karachi became the land of the Muhajirs, a land they built and watered with their blood.

Today, it has been 77 years since Pakistan was created and 53 years since the birth of Bangladesh. And what have we gained? We are still empty-handed. If we raise our eyes and look around, we won't find even a single person who can eradicate the seeds of hatred, not a single leader who can truly work to improve the life of an ordinary person.

The story I am writing teaches us an important lesson that in this very world, we reap what we sow. Life is no coincidence; a person's actions are a reflection of their character. If our sense of identity our "Qaumiyat" (Nationality) were based on love and humanity rather than narrow divisions, this world would be nothing less than paradise. But sadly, that is not the case.

We all belong to this earth some of us were left on one side of the border, some on the other. Some became victims of religion, others of nationalism. So why not unite again? Why not speak a common language a language of love, compassion, and humanity? Why not talk about friendship, which we need as much as this time does? Why should we pass on a legacy of hatred to the next generation? Why not light a lamp of love from this story and lay the first brick of compassion in our region?

Let us learn a lesson from this tale of conflict and begin a new journey of love with the people of India, Pakistan, and Bangladesh, so that no one ever again becomes a prisoner of war in their own homeland.

This land has witnessed too much. India was divided, Pakistan was born, and then Bangladesh. The fabric of identity was torn apart. The debate continues and will continue over who broke the country: the "Two-Nation Theory" or politics? And the most tragic part is that, even today, we are unable to decide who was responsible for the breakup of Pakistan, language, nationalism, or a political defeat or perhaps a political conspiracy.

****

CONTENTS

LINE OF PAIN

While walking through the market today, my eyes suddenly landed on the showcase of a toy shop, and I froze. My feet moved unconsciously toward the store. I asked the shopkeeper about the Magic Slate that caught my attention.

I stood still, staring at it, and memories linked to that slate began to play before my eyes like a film. I became so absorbed that I forgot everything around me.

Suddenly, a voice startled me. The shopkeeper repeatedly asked, “Madam, would you like to buy this slate?” I handed it back and said no, then stepped out, finished the rest of my shopping, and headed home. But somewhere in the back of my mind, that slate lingered.

My past kept playing in my head like a movie, my childhood, Bangladesh, riots, chaos, war, corpses, blood, civil unrest, imprisonment, and then independence.

All of it came rushing back like a haunting dream. That slate had dragged me back into a past I wanted to forget or thought I had forgotten.

It's been 77 years since India and Pakistan were created, and 53 years since the birth of Bangladesh, but when I reflect, it all feels like it happened just yesterday.

The circumstances and events that marked my childhood, especially during those two and a half years, taught me what fear, captivity, and survival mean. That experience taught me humanity. If I am a social worker today, it is because of that war.

It taught me to love people and hate hatred. I learned what death looks like and what it means to crave life after seeing it up close. I understood hunger and learned the true meaning of helplessness.

For the past 34 years, I have been living here in India, proudly holding my Indian nationality, because I came here as a bride. I see both countries this way: Pakistan is my *Maika* (maternal home), and India is my *Sasural* (in-laws' home). And if you look from my parents' side, India is my original homeland.

I still remember how overjoyed I was when I received my Indian citizenship certificate. But there was also a pain a realization that now I'd have to stand in visa queues to meet my parents, my siblings. That pain is something I know all too well.

Every year, the struggle to get a visa to meet my loved ones is agonizing. I couldn't attend my brother's or my sister's wedding. I couldn't see my father before he passed. Nor could my mother, brothers, or sisters come for my daughter Mahin's or son Yusuf's weddings. They could not share in my joys or my sorrows. I hope that perhaps my mother will be able to attend my younger son Ismail's wedding if fate allows.

There are thousands of women like me who, after the war of independence, married across borders. These women belong to all communities.

The Partition might have drawn geographic boundaries, but it could never divide hearts, families, or relationships. Even today, you can see people waiting outside the Indian and Pakistani embassies, desperately seeking visas to meet their loved ones. Why do they endure humiliation, pain, pleading, and tears for that visa? Why do they long to come to India or go to Pakistan? Why do parents still marry off their daughters across the border? Has anyone ever asked them?

Let me answer: because memories are tied there, children were left behind, and relationships were torn apart. That bond is what they are trying to keep alive. They want an excuse to return, to see the land where their childhood unfolded a land that now feels lost to them. And this cycle will continue until the last living person who endured Partition and the Bangladesh war is gone.

I've had many unforgettable moments in my life. On 22 December 2003, my brother Rehan was getting married. I had a visa but couldn't get a flight ticket because all flights were suspended and only buses were running. Despite all efforts, I couldn't make it. Oddly enough, I had managed to send all the gifts to him by courier, so he got those gifts, but I didn't make it. I remember sitting in a cinema hall during his *nikah*, watching *Kal Ho Naa Ho*, quietly crying in the dark, hiding my tears. If flights hadn't been suspended, I would've been there.

On 13 February 2004, my younger sister Fouzia got married and again I couldn't attend, for the same reason, no flights.

Then, on 13 January 2013, my father passed away. I couldn't get a visa and missed the chance to see him one last time. He called out to me from the ICU via Skype, and then he was gone.

The fourth time was on 29 December 2016, my daughter Mahin's wedding, the biggest joy of my life. Visa policies had become so strict by then that, despite every attempt, my brothers, sisters, and mother couldn't attend.

And again, on 23 December 2021, during my elder son Yusuf's wedding, the visa became the reason for their absence.

Finally, after 13 years, on 18 November 2023, I went to Dubai and met my elder sister, and on 24 November 2023, I met my mother and sisters in Dammam (Saudi Arabia).

There are so many women like me suffering in silence. If only people could understand our pain.

Even today, whenever I see news of war, riots, floods, or earthquakes, when I see children crying or orphaned, when I see them suffering from hunger and thirst, my own childhood flashes before my eyes, and I cry.

Whether it's war or chaos in any part of the world, I can't bear to watch. That's why I avoid the news and newspapers. My children say I'm too emotional. But how can I explain to them what I feel when I see wounded children, grieving women, and broken youth? It feels like I'm reliving all the pain and trauma again.

That slate today reopened my old wounds and reaffirmed my commitment.

I am grateful to my parents who helped me put this story together. They had to build a home three times. I don't complain to God. He always gives us more than before. But think about it, even once, gathering every straw to build a home is hard. Here, we were uprooted and rebuilt our lives *three times*.

I vividly remember that in 1984, when the Muhajir Qaumi Movement gained momentum and tensions flared between Sindhis and Muhajirs, my father was terrified. He began gathering important documents and valuables in one place, fearing another civil war, another displacement. Even today, we live with the fear of war.

But from that war, I learned a lesson never get too attached to material things. A person's greatest wealth is their education, their values, their love for humanity, and trust in God, who always helps them find their place again. Education and skill are the only wealth that no one can take from you. And they never let a person go hungry.

****

FAMILY

Before coming to the main story, it would be better if I share some details about my family. Our ancestors, Abdul Ghafoor Khan's forefathers, were originally from the town of "Wana" in the South Waziristan district of the Dera Ismail Khan Division, who later settled in the city of "Birnawan" in Bihar. On my paternal grandmother's side, my great-grandfather, "Mian Khan," was also from Dera Ismail Khan and had settled in Patna. We no longer know where their ancestral homes and graves are located.

My esteemed great-grandfather, Abdul Ghafoor Khan, was born in "Birnawan" (Bihar) and was one of the prominent and respected landowners there. My grandfather, Dr. Shams-uz-Zama Khan, was also born in "Birnawan." After my grandfather became a doctor, he married my grandmother, Maimoona Khatoon, who was also from a Pashtun background and lived in "Sanowli" (Bihar).

Since my grandfather was a doctor by profession, his postings were in various cities, including "Neura (Bihar). Alongside his medical career, my grandfather was also a landowner, which gave him respect and recognition in the community. Our ancestral home was in "Birnawan," where my father and his siblings were raised.

The upbringing of my father and his brothers and sisters was in our ancestral mansion in "Birnawan," which, for its time, was quite grand. There were fields for agriculture, orchards for mangoes, and ponds for fish farming. In short, there was no shortage of anything, from fruits to vegetables and grains.

My late father, Shamim Ahmad Khan, had four brothers and three sisters, whose names were as follows: Shafi Ahmad Khan, Dr. Rafi Ahmad Khan, Shamim Ahmad Khan, Naseem Ahmad Khan, Saleha Khatoon, Saeeda Khatoon, and Wajida Khatoon.

My grandmother Maimoona Khatoon was a homemaker. My eldest uncle, Shafi Ahmad Khan, and his wife passed away within a few years of their marriage due to tuberculosis, as there was no treatment for it at that time. As a result of their deaths, their only daughter also passed away at the age of two. My uncle, Dr. Rafi Ahmad Khan (may he rest in peace), who was a doctor by profession, along with his wife (may she rest in peace), moved to Pakistan, where their children still live.

My third uncle, Naseem Ahmad Khan, had a political background and was a well-known and compassionate man of his time. Unfortunately, due to family discord and internal enmity, he was killed on his land in Purnia. His eldest son was also killed along with him. A few years after my uncle's death, his second son also lost his life due to a family dispute.

However, the remaining children of my uncle are thriving in Purnia, living happily and successfully.

My eldest aunt, Saleha Khatoon, got married in Bhagalpur. My uncle, Farooq, owned a mustard oil mill. After the passing of Aunt Saleha (may she rest in peace), my grandfather arranged the marriage of Aunt Saeeda (may she rest in peace) to Uncle Farooq so that Saleha's children could receive the love of a mother from their aunt.

My youngest aunt (may she rest in peace), Wajda, was married to Dr. Moeen Khan, who later moved to Bangladesh and then to Pakistan.

My father (may he rest in peace) was an electrical engineer by profession. His early education was in "Birnawan," followed by "Neura," and finally in "Patna." My father worked for Patna Electric Supply during his career.

My great-grandfather, Ismail Khan, was a landowner and considered one of Patna's respected individuals. His name was also well-known and recognized in political and social circles; even today, people mention his name with respect.

My great-grandfather, Ismail Khan, had three marriages; from one, he had three sons and four daughters. The sons were Yusuf Khan, Ilyas Khan, and Idrees Khan, and the four daughters were Qamar-un-Nisa, Akhtar-un-Nisa, Ashraf-un-Nisa, and Zeenat-un-Nisa.

My maternal grandfather, Yusuf Khan, was a businessman by profession. He owned a leather bag shop in Patna Market and was involved in the leather business. He married my grandmother, Anisa Khatoon, who belonged to a town called

'Mai' near the city of Gaya in Bihar. Her father, Anayat Khan, was a landowner in a village called 'Mai', located in the Gaya district of Bihar. She has three sisters Zubaida, Haseena, Jameela and one brother named Murtaza Khan.

My grandfather Yusuf Khan passed away six months after the marriage. At that time, my grandmother Anisa Khatoon was pregnant, and my mother, Najma Khanum, had not yet been born.

My grandmother was a modest and devoted wife who spent her entire life in her in-laws' home after her husband's death, just so that her daughter could know her father and his family.

My mother, Najma-un-Nisa Khanum, was born in Ismail Manzil in Sabzi Bagh. She was raised and received her early education under the care of her grandfather, Ismail Khan, who brought her up with great love. After the death of her grandfather, Ismail Khan, when she was six years old, her upbringing was taken over by her uncles.

My mother was very eager to go to school, but in those days, girls from respectable families did not attend school, so she was never able to go. Her early education took place at home. Being very intelligent, my mother learned many things just by observing. She was fluent in both Urdu and Bengali, and she could also read and write English.

In short, both my father and mother came from very noble and respected families. I am not saying this to boast about my family, but because, as the story unfolds, you will see how the wheel of time turns.

At the age of 16, Najma Khanam (my mother) marriage was arranged with Shamim Ahmed Khan (my father). My father was considered one of the handsome young men of his time. He was six feet tall, had a wheatish complexion, an attractive face, a lively personality, and a cheerful nature. He had a taste for good food and stylish clothes, and he also enjoyed traveling. People even used to call him 'Film Star Rajendra Kumar.' He was very fond of football and was also a player.

My mother was a delicate woman of medium height, blessed with good looks and a commanding presence, like that of a typical Pashtun woman. She was considered one of the beautiful women of her time and was given the title of 'The Full Moon of the Fourteenth Night' in her in-laws' home.

My parents were married on October 22, 1961. My father was an electrical engineer and got a job with the Patna Electric Supply. After the wedding, my mother stayed for a while in Birnawa with her in-laws. Later, when my father rented a house in Langar Toli, Patna, he brought my mother there to live with him.

Just a few months into their marriage, my youngest paternal aunt, Wajida Phuppi, and her husband, Dr. Moin Khan (my uncle), decided to move to Dhaka in search of better job opportunities and a brighter future. At that time, Dhaka was still part of East Pakistan. Sometime after settling there, my aunt returned for a visit and began persuading my father. She told him there was nothing left for him here and encouraged him to come to Dhaka, where he could start his own business.

She mentioned that her husband's clinic was already doing very well. Swayed by her words, my father made a bold decision, he left his job at the Patna Electric Supply and decided to try his luck in East Pakistan. Despite my grandfather and other family members warning him against it, he turned his back on a property worth a million and set out on this new journey.

That twist of fate set our parents on the path of migration. Once again, a new generation of our family left behind their homeland, their city, their people, and a life of comfort and luxury.

They set out to embrace a place that perhaps had never truly been theirs, a land whose soil held neither love nor loyalty.

****

MIGRATION

After the War of Independence, the migration of Muslims leaving India continued well into the 1960s. Families from cities across India moved to East and West Pakistan in search of brighter futures.

My *Phuppi Jaan* (aunt) was among those early migrants. She didn't just go alone she took my father and uncle along with her. A few years into her marriage, she moved to Dhaka.

When her husband's business prospered, she persuaded my father (Abbi) to follow. In 1962, he left for Dhaka, entrusting my mother (Ammi) to the care of my grandmother (Anisa Khatoon) at Ismail Manzil. I'll go ahead, he promised, make arrangements, and then call for you.

My Abbi journeyed across the Bay of Bengal and arrived in Dhaka the same route many hopeful families took back then. Once he had assessed the situation and secured a place to stay, he sent word for Ammi. A family man at heart, he found life unbearable without her.

Coincidentally, my younger aunt (Wajida Phuppi) was planning a visit back to India to see my grandparents. Abbi asked her to bring Ammi along. And so, Ammi, crossed the Bay of Bengal and joined him in East Pakistan, stepping into what would become a new chapter in their lives.

It was a strange, unfamiliar world, a new place, new people. The language was foreign, the customs different. The comforts and luxuries they had once known were gone. For a while, they stayed with relatives.

Abbi found work, but neither he nor Ammi felt at home. Abbi regretted leaving his secure job at Patna Electric Supply, and Ammi longed deeply for her mother's (Nani) embrace.

Their discontent grew, especially as Ammi prepared for the birth of my elder sister. They contemplated returning to India, but family and friends advised against it. What will you do back there now? You no longer have a job, and there's no future waiting for you. Reluctantly, they decided to stay. But fate had other plans.

One day, without warning, Abbi lost his job. Anxiety consumed both my parents. Despite tireless efforts, no new opportunity came his way. Finally, Abbi wrote to my grandfather, asking for financial help.

During this difficult time, my maternal grandmother (Nani) also arrived from India to be with her daughter. Soon after, my grandfather (Shams-uz-Zama Khan) came too, bringing 20,000 rupees and, more importantly, the reassurance only a father can give.

Despite his pleas for Abbi to return home, Abbi remained steadfast. Reluctantly, my grandfather handed him the money, a lifeline to start a business.

That money became a turning point. Abbi established Samina Trading Company, named after my elder sister, Samina Khanam, who was born soon after.

Because of my Abbi's past engineering work in Dhaka, he had built strong connections. Soon, major companies began awarding him contracts. Life steadied. As prosperity returned, he rented a large house near Dhaka Town Hall in Mohammadpur, for 150 rupees a month.

We lived upstairs. The ground floor was home to Ammi's cousin, Ashfaq Mamoon, and his sister, Zaibun Khala, with their families.

Abbi, ever a man of refined taste, spared no expense in making our house a home. Ammi had four household helpers who managed the chores and looked after us children. My grandmother (Anisa Khatoon) lived with us, too.

The house was spacious, a dining room, a guest room, two bedrooms, a kitchen, and wide courtyards on both sides. All the comforts of the world surrounded us once again. Life was peaceful and full of joy.

But as the saying goes, God's plans are always for the best, even when we don't understand them. The trials ahead were meant to prepare us for challenges we could not yet foresee.

It wasn't until much later, when we were released from captivity as prisoners of war, that we understood the wisdom behind the hardships we once found so bitter.

One day, as usual, Abbi set out to meet a client, a meeting that promised to secure the biggest contract of his career. On the way, he passed a beggar. He often helped those in need, but pressed for time, he hurried past. Still, guilt tugged at his heart.

Moments later, in his rush to avoid a passerby, his scooter slipped. His right leg shattered above the knee.

He was rushed to the hospital. The renowned Dr. Jamali performed an extensive surgery, inserting a rod to hold the broken bone together. The rod would remain in his leg for a year. The healing was slow and painful.

The business suffered. Abbi had applied for a phone line, but it hadn't been installed yet. All calls came to the relative's downstairs. In the first fifteen days of his hospitalization, neither my parents nor his clients received any communication. One by one, his clients drifted away.

Six months passed. Abbi lay bedridden. The thriving business began to collapse. Soon, we were struggling even for basic necessities.

We were just three children then my sister Samina, my brother Nadeem, and me. My grandmother (Nani) was still with us. Day by day, our situation worsened. Relatives, once supportive, began to distance themselves.

In desperation, Ammi reached out to my grandfather once more. He arrived with 25,000 rupees, which helped us survive for a while. But Abbi, once so proud and successful, was now using crutches, his spirit broken.

Yet Ammi never gave up. Each day, she scanned the newspapers for job openings. One day, she found an advertisement from Pakistan International Airlines (P.I.A). They needed electrical engineers in East Pakistan.

She urged Abbi to apply. He refused at first, but after much persuasion from Ammi and Nani, he submitted his application. Fifteen days passed with no response.

Then, one morning, Ammi woke with a dream. She saw a white envelope bordered in green, marked with the letters "P.I.A." Abbi dismissed it as mere fantasy.

But that very evening, the postman arrived carrying an envelope identical to the one from her dream. Inside was an interview call letter.

Though nervous about attending the interview on crutches especially after recently having the iron plate removed from his leg. Abbi encouraged by Ammi and Nani, agreed to go. He dressed in his usual white clothes and set out with Ammi by his side.

At the interview, after waiting long hours, his wound began to bleed again. He tried to hide it with a handkerchief. But the interviewer who, by coincidence, shared Abbi's name told him gently, there's no need to hide it. Just tell us how long until the stitches come out and how soon you can resume work.

The interview lasted fifteen minutes. Abbi returned home disheartened. Ammi reassured him, you will get this job. I know it.

A week later, Ammi had another dream the same envelope, with the same promise of good news. Abbi smiled sadly, why give me false hope?

But once again, the postman brought the envelope she had seen in her dream. Abbi had been selected. He was to start in a month.

Still, he hesitated. The salary was only 700 rupees, a far cry from the earnings he once commanded. How can we manage on so little? he asked.

But Ammi wisely said, It's better than nothing. At least it's steady until you find something better. At last, he agreed.

On the first day of his new job, he promised to return in two hours. Four hours passed. Ammi anxiously paced the balcony.

Finally, two auto-rickshaws arrived, both filled to the brim with groceries and supplies. Abbi stepped out, beaming. You were right. I made the right decision.

Confused, Ammi asked how he managed to buy so much when they had so little.

Smiling, he explained, yes, the salary is 700 rupees. But it comes with free monthly rations, weekly supplies of milk, eggs, biscuits, bread, jam, and fruit. Medical care is free. Air travel is free. And today, as soon as I got my coupons, I collected everything for the house.

It was, as he described, a royal job, rich in blessings, not just income.

Life found its rhythm once more. Prosperity returned, and with it, peace. Abbi even bought a car, too fearful now to ride a scooter. The house had a phone line.

We lacked for nothing. Food, medicine, and even travel was no longer concerns. God had provided more than we had ever imagined.

Years passed. Dhaka became home. Our neighbourhood near the Town Hall was filled with grand houses and well-off families. Even today, I remember those childhood days vividly. Some memories, they say, remain etched in the heart forever.

Across from our home, beside the neighbouring house, stood two magnificent trees, a towering peepal and a sprawling tamarind. Their yard was covered in soft, earthen soil, which the family carefully coated with smooth clay every week.

We children loved that patch of earth. Every evening, we would gather there, marking the ground with chalk to play ek cut, do cut. I'm not sure what children call it nowadays, but back then, it was the highlight of our days.

As we played, the elderly woman who lived in that house, whom we affectionately called Imli Wali Nani, would scold us. You little rascals, she'd say, shaking her head. Don't draw lines on the ground. It takes away the blessings and ruins homes.

At the time, we dismissed her words as the superstitions of the old. But in the years to come, as war scattered families and homes fell silent, I often thought back to her warning. Perhaps there had been a grain of truth in her fears.

Next door to us lived a man we children called Police Wale Uncle. Abbi had generously extended our electricity connection to his home. But his children and we rarely got along.

Whenever a quarrel broke out, as they often did, we mischievously unplugged their power line. Abbi would scold us severely each time.

Because the man was stout, in our childish anger, we secretly called him Moto Seth. His family was unusual.

Each night, he and his children would sneak around the neighbourhood, collecting bricks from construction sites. By day, they would carefully stack those bricks, slowly building rooms. Over time, they managed to construct three rooms, topped with tin roofs.

Though the bricks may have been "borrowed," the land was their own. They were building a home for their future, blissfully unaware of what destiny held.

Beside their modest home stood the grandest house in our neighbourhood, a three-story building where three brothers and their large families lived. Most of their children were boys, except for one girl.

Her name was **Saba**, and I remember it to this day. As the only daughter, her every wish was fulfilled in an instant.

Her doll's wedding remains one of my most vivid memories. The event was no less elaborate than a real wedding.

Five hundred guests were invited. The celebrations lasted five days. We all brought our dolls, while Saba's cousins arrived with a groom doll's procession, complete with music and fanfare. No real bride, I believe, ever had such a grand celebration in those days.

Directly across from our home lived Mohan Uncle, a young man back then.

He had an uncle, known to us only as Mohan's Mamoo. We never learned his real name. Ammi and my aunt (Nasim Mami) called him by that affectionate title, and so did we.

Whether his mind was light or he simply carried a carefree spirit, I don't know. But his antics were a constant source of amusement for everyone.

After finishing their daily chores, Ammi and Nasim Mami (Aunt) would sit together in the balcony, watching his comical behaviour.

Whenever he returned from shopping, he would bang loudly on the door until he was sure that the neighbourhood Bhabhi's had noticed him.

During his wedding, every step from dressing as the groom to bringing home his bride was announced at full volume so no one could miss it.

Even after marriage, whenever he took his wife out, he would stand outside the door, calling loudly, "Chalogi? Chalogi? Chalogi?" (Will you come? Will you come for an outing?)

Our lives were filled with these sweet and sour moments, the simple joys and oddities of neighbourhood life.

You might wonder why I tell you about these people. It's because they were not just neighbours. They were part of our lives, our shared joys and sorrows. And in the dark days that followed, what happened to each of them became part of the story that cannot be left untold.

Life flowed on in its colourful, cheerful way. Everywhere we looked, it felt like springtime. Nothing was lacking. Our home was once again filled with every comfort. Picnics, parties, and childhood games were in full swing.

Among us lived a young Bengali boy named Abdul. He had no family. My parents had taken him in, raising him as one of their own. Officially, he was a helper, but in truth, he was a part of the family. My parents loved him like a son. He was twelve years old.

In Dhaka, we never thought of ourselves as Khan, Bihari, or Bengali. People lived together with such warmth that no one bothered with caste or origin.

But perhaps fate had more tests waiting for us. Many chapters of life some harsh, some bittersweets were still to unfold.

****

FALL OF DHAKA

Dhaka thrived in its rhythm, a city pulsing with life. Its people went about their days, absorbed in the routines and joys that made up their world. But beneath the surface, change was gathering like a distant storm. Without warning, the fabric of East Pakistan began to unravel.

The reasons were rooted deep in politics, though for the ordinary families filling the streets, it was difficult to grasp at first.

Geography had betrayed them from the beginning. East and West Pakistan, separated by more than a thousand miles of foreign land, had been an uneasy union from the start. And now, frustrations simmered. The people of East Pakistan grew restless under what they perceived as the dismissive and unequal attitude of their western counterparts.

Economics added fuel to the fire. Cultural divides deepened the cracks. And language that most personal marker of identity became the breaking point. The West insisted on Urdu as the national language. The East clung fiercely to

Bengali. Neither side was willing to yield, and the gap widened into a chasm.

Politics became a game of shadows. Elections stirred hope and then crushed it. Day by day, tension thickened like smoke in the air.

The city that had once been a cradle of harmony now stood on the edge of something no one could yet name but all could feel.

As the city's unrest worsened, Abbi made the difficult decision to send us to Karachi. He gathered the family and brought us all to what he hoped would be safer ground.

In Karachi's near Karimabad area, a new apartment complex had just been completed Al-Azam Square. It was a modern marvel at the time, thoughtfully designed with gardens between every two blocks.

The moment Abbi saw it, he knew it would be the right place for us. He rented a flat, and soon, we had a new home.

Our family, Ammi, Nani, eldest sister Samina, myself (Rozina), younger brother Nadeem, little sister Nazia, and baby Rehan settled into this new life.

Abbi enrolled Samina Appa and me at Delhi Public School, close to our building. We were placed in Nursery and L.K.G. Every day, a kind woman would escort us to school, crossing the railway tracks that separated us from the campus.

Nadeem was still too young for school. Rehan was an infant, and Nazia had just turned one. The two youngest were so close in age that Nani cared for Nazia while Ammi looked after Rehan.

Once we were settled, Abbi returned to Dhaka to continue his work. He had made sure that both our homes the one in Karachi and the one back in Dhaka were well-furnished and comfortable.

But despite the new surroundings, Ammi's heart remained heavy. Anxiety lingered in the corners of her mind, refusing to fade.

Abbi tried to reassure Ammi. There's nothing to worry about, he said gently. My ticket is free, I can come whenever I like, or call you all to visit me as soon as things settle down. And you're not alone. Amma (Nani) and the children are with you.

But Ammi's eyes, filled with quiet longing, betrayed the ache in her heart. I know, she whispered, but my heart stays with you.

Abbi smiled softly, though his own eyes carried the same unspoken heaviness.

My heart doesn't feel at ease without the children either. Just be patient a little longer. Let the elections pass. Let things calm down.

They both knew patience would be their only companion in the uncertain days ahead.

After Abbi returned to Dhaka, Ammi immersed herself in the world of her children.

Karachi was peaceful then its population still small, its neighbourhoods quiet and calm. For a woman who had never stepped much beyond her home from Patna to Dhaka, always surrounded by household help Karachi was a new experience.

Now, everything fell to her. An *ayah* took my sister and me to and from school and helped with the housework.

In Dhaka, Abdul had managed Abbi's errands, and two Bengali maids took care of the household. But here, Ammi became both the homemaker and the manager of all things inside and out.

Yet she adapted with grace. Ammi had always been a social woman. Friendships blossomed easily around her. In those days, neighbours-built bonds not just with words but with the exchange of home-cooked dishes a tray of biryani, a bowl of halwa, a sign of warmth and welcome.

Just as she had in Dhaka, Ammi quickly made friends here too. Every evening, she would take us to the park. While we played, she shared light-hearted conversations with the other mothers. Soon, the neighbourhood became like an extended family, and many of her burdens were lightened by the kindness of those around her.

We children thrived in this new city. There was a garden to explore, swings to ride, and new friends to play with.

During this time, Abbi visited us twice, each visit a joyful reminder that though we were apart, the family was still whole.

Ammi found comfort in knowing we now had homes in both cities.

We proudly told our new friends that we had flown to Karachi by airplane, and that our Abbi still travelled back and forth by plane. But sometimes, late at night or during quiet moments, we all found ourselves missing the Dhaka house. Missing Dhaka itself.

And so, six to eight months passed in this rhythm of new beginnings and lingering memories.

Then, one day, without warning, Abbi arrived in Karachi. As soon as he entered the house, there was a familiar warmth in his eyes, but also a quiet urgency.

I can't bear it anymore; he told my Ammi. My heart just doesn't settle without you and the children. Prepare to return to Dhaka. The Pakistan Army has arrived there now. The situation is under control.

Ammi looked at him with worry. I've settled everything here, she said softly. There's so much household stuff now, the children are settled in school. And things still don't feel completely safe.

Abbi took her hands gently. The situation *is* better, and besides, I can't concentrate on work when I'm constantly worrying about you all. It's best if we stay together.

Ammi was quiet for a moment. Then she nodded slowly.

Alright. I'll withdraw the children from school. I'll also need to inform the landlord. As for the dishes and other heavy items, I'll leave them with Bhabhi, (Nasim Mami who used to live below us in Dhaka. She's now moved Karachi and has built her own house.)

Good, Abbi said with relief. Do whatever needs to be done and let me know. I'll arrange the tickets through my office. From now on, whatever joys and hardships come, we'll face them together.

Ammi smiled faintly, a mixture of hope and fear in her eyes. Alright. I'll take care of everything. I'll come with you. The rest is in God's hands.

And with that decision, the family prepared once again to return to Dhaka unaware of the storm that lay ahead.

Just as Abbi's accident had carried a hidden wisdom only God could see, so too did Ammi's decision to store the essential household items in Karachi.

We, as mere humans, could not grasp what the Almighty had already written. As the saying goes, no one can escape what is destined. Whatever is meant to happen will unfold, no matter how much we try to change its course, and so it was with us.

We had been safe, settled, and thriving in Karachi. But Abbi's growing anxiety had drawn us back to Dhaka, back to the place where, unknown to us, a long and difficult chapter was waiting to be written. A new chain of hardships was poised to begin.

Once again, Ammi gave up the comfortable home she had built in Karachi and returned with us to our familiar house in Dhaka.

For a brief while, the city seemed calmer. Life found a fragile normalcy. We were enrolled in school once more.

We children, of course, returned to our playful mischief, but this time, our freedom came with limits. We were no longer allowed to roam outside as freely as before. The situation is not stable, we were warned. Stay close to home.

Abbi now owns two vehicles. One was a small car, a Foxy, and the other, a van we often used for family picnics.

He kept both vehicles fuelled at all times. “In case of emergency,” he said quietly, “I don’t want to worry about finding petrol.”

Even though life seemed to have returned to its usual patterns, there was an unspoken tension in the air like the hush before a storm.

A strange tension had settled over the city. An unease that seemed to hum beneath every conversation, every glance exchanged between neighbours.

The Mukti Bahini activities had surged, and the Pakistani Army was cracking down, rounding up suspected members wherever they could be found. The atmosphere grew heavier with each passing day.

Even the once-friendly Bengali families in the neighbourhood had become distant, their words clipped, their expressions guarded.

To one side of our home still lived the Police Wale Uncle and his family. On the other side stood a grand house belonging to a Bengali Muslim family who now lived in Karachi. Their house remained locked and silent.

Nasim Mami had moved to Karachi as well, while Zebun Khala and her children continued living downstairs in their part of the house.

Everywhere, the tension grew thicker, as though the very air had changed.

The Pakistani Army's actions against Mukti Bahini had set the entire neighbourhood on edge.

One evening, Abbi's friend Rehman Sahib, a Bengali man who also worked at P.I.A arrived at our door with his wife. Their faces were pale, drawn tight with worry. They had always been close to our family. But today, they carried the weight of desperation.

Shamim, Rehman Uncle said, his voice trembling. I'm in serious trouble. I need your help.

Abbi motioned for them to sit. Please, Rehman Bhai, calm down. Have some water. Tell me what's wrong.

Rehman Uncle gripped the glass tightly but didn't drink. His eyes, usually so calm, now brimmed with fear.

The Army, he said hoarsely. They've taken both my sons. They believe they were working for the Mukti Bahini.

A cold hush fell over the room. Even as a child, I could feel the heaviness of the moment.

Trouble, the kind that changed lives forever, had come to someone we knew. And somehow, we all sensed this was only the beginning.

Abbi leaned forward, his voice calm but firm. Do you know where they've taken your sons?

Rehman Uncle shook his head helplessly. I've searched everywhere. I've asked everyone I could. No one knows. It seems they've been taken to an unknown location.

Abbi nodded slowly, the weight of the situation sinking in. I'll try to help, he said. I do know some of the Army officers, men for whom I've done electrical work. I'll see if I can reach them. If I can meet with someone, I'll talk to them. You know how things are these days.

Rehman Uncle grasped my father's hand, eyes shining with gratitude. Please, just try. The rest is in God's hands. I'll be forever grateful to you.

My sons, Rehman Uncle said, his voice breaking, are like your own sons, Shamim. You know they would never get involved in anything dangerous.

Without wasting another moment, Abbi took Rehman Uncle with him. He asked Auntie to stay behind with Ammi and Nani.

Ammi and Nani comforted her gently, speaking soothing words, though everyone in the room knew how uncertain comfort could be in such dangerous times.

It took great difficulty and determination, but at last, Abbi managed to secure a meeting with an officer of the Pakistani Army.

When the officer arrived, Abbi respectfully explained everything, how Rehman Uncle's sons had been taken, how they were sure it was a misunderstanding, and how desperate the family was for any word of their whereabouts.

Abbi asked, not just as a friend, but as a father himself, pleading for their help.

Sir, I know Rehman Sahib well. He's an honest man. His sons are like my own. This must be some mistake.

When Abbi met the Army officer, he spoke with quiet conviction.

The officer listened patiently but shook his head. His face was serious, his tone cautious.

First of all, he said, I don't even know who picked them up or where they were taken. If action was taken, there must have been solid information behind it.

Abbi leaned forward, refusing to give up. Please, at least try to find out. It could be a misunderstanding. There are thousands of boys with the same names. It's possible they were taken by mistake.

The officer asked for their descriptions. He wrote down every detail and finally said, I'll see what I can do. But I can't promise anything.

Abbi and Rehman Uncle returned home with heavy heart. Auntie's sobs echoed through the house. Ammi and Nani sat beside her, offering whatever comfort they could, though their words felt so small against such a vast fear.

After Rehman Uncle and Auntie left, Ammi turned to Abbi, worry in her eyes.

What do you think? Do you believe they'll be found?

Abbi exhaled slowly, the lines on his face deeper than before.

We'll see, he said. This is an Army operation. And they're Bengalis; the Mukti Bahini connection is serious. But if God has destined their rescue through my hands, then they'll be found.

Ammi hesitated, then asked softly, and if they were part of the Mukti Bahini?

Abbi shook his head. I don't believe it. I've met both boys. They are decent, respectful young men. This feels like a mistake.

The tension in our home was no longer just about strangers or distant conflicts.

It was now the fear of what could happen to friends, and what might one day happen to us.

The next day, Abbi and Rehman Uncle returned to meet the Army officer. He had summoned them personally.

The officer held Abbi in high regard, not only because of his honesty but because Abbi had often helped him with electrical work at his private residence.

When they arrived, the officer greeted them briefly, then motioned for Abbi to step aside.

Tell me, Shamim Sahib, he asked quietly, are you sure that Rehman's sons aren't involved in anything?

Abbi hesitated, choosing his words carefully. Sir, I can't say with absolute certainty. But I've met both boys. They seem like decent, well-mannered young men. They often visit our home. I've never seen anything suspicious.

The officer nodded gravely. There's something you should know. His voice dropped to a serious, almost weary tone.

The boys have been accused of smuggling weapons.

A chill ran through my Abbi. What will happen now, Sir? What should I tell their father?

Without answering directly, the officer gestured for Abbi to follow him. Together, they walked back to where Rehman Uncle waited, his face pale with dread.

Standing before him, the officer said bluntly, Rehman, I've found your sons. Both have been accused of smuggling arms, a very serious charge.

Rehman Uncle's face crumpled with disbelief. No! he cried, his hands folded in desperate pleading. That's not true. I swear to you, my sons would never do such a thing. Please, Sir. They're innocent. His voice broke, and silent tears streamed down his face.

The room fell into a heavy silence, the weight of the accusation pressing down on everyone. What had begun as a hopeful search for answers was quickly becoming something far darker.

The officer took a long breath. I'm trying, he said. Both of you, wait here. I'll be back.

With that, he disappeared through a door, leaving Abbi and Rehman Uncle standing in anxious silence.

Time seemed to stretch endlessly. They exchanged no words, only the silent, shared fear of fathers who had done all they could.

At last, the officer returned. His expression was unreadable.

Come with me, he said.

Abbi, the officer, and Rehman Uncle followed him through narrow lanes and guarded passages until they reached the place where the boys were being held.

At the gate, the officer turned. Stay here, he instructed, and went inside alone.

Minutes dragged into what felt like hours.

Finally, the officer reappeared, and with him, Rehman Uncle's two sons.

The relief in the air was so thick it was almost suffocating.

The officer spoke firmly, but not unkindly. Here they are. Your sons. But warn them, be careful. These are dangerous times. We won't be able to help again.

Before anyone could say a word, Rehman Uncle collapsed to the ground, pressing his forehead into the dirt in a deep **sajda** of gratitude. His tears soaked the earth as he murmured prayers and thanks.

Then he rose, clasping the officer's hands. Thank you, thank you. You've saved my sons. You've saved my family.

The officer simply nodded, his face stern but perhaps a little softer than before.

And Abbi stood quietly beside them, his heart full, knowing he had done what any father and friend would do, though the danger was far from over.

The officer looked at Rehman Uncle with steady eyes.

Rehman Sahib, give thanks to God, and to Shamim Sahib, whom God made a means for this. And tell your sons, if they have even the slightest connection to the Mukti Bahini, they must leave it behind. Luck does not favour a man twice.

Abbi thanked the officer sincerely and left with Rehman Uncle.

When they returned home, Aunty was waiting anxiously. The moment she saw her sons, she was overwhelmed with joy, embracing them with tears streaming down her face. She could hardly believe they were safe and standing before her.

That evening, Rehman Uncle gathered his sons close. His voice was gentle but firm.

My sons, he said, you must thank Shamim Uncle. It's because of him that your lives were spared. You have a new beginning now, never forget this favour.

Abbi shook his head humbly. No, he said softly. I did nothing. It is God who does everything. He only chooses people as instruments. Life and death are in His hands alone.

And indeed, it was true. God had chosen Abbi as the means, not only to save Rehman Uncle's sons but, in time, to protect our own family from the trials yet to come.

Before leaving, Rehman Uncle took Abbi's hand solemnly.

Shamim Bhai, he said, I give you my word, if ever, in this life, hardship finds you and you need anything from me, just call. I will come, no matter what.

In that moment, looking at the faces around the room, my parents, Rehman Uncle, his wife, and their sons, there was a happiness deeper than words.

A happiness born from love, humanity, and the bonds of brotherhood that no storm could easily break.

By then, the atmosphere in Dhaka, and indeed, all of East Pakistan, had shifted into something dark and unpredictable.

The once invisible line between Bengali and non-Bengali had sharpened into a deep, dangerous divide.

The Bengali Muslims had formed their own militia, known as the Mukti Bahini. In response, the non-Bengali community had organized a Razakar group called Badr.

Day by day, life for ordinary families like ours became more difficult, more uncertain. Fear crept into every household. No one could guess what the next day would bring.

Sometimes the Army would raid neighbourhoods, taking away young men suspected of fighting for Mukti Bahini. Other times, Mukti Bahini fighters would abduct boys from the Badr group.

Rumors spread like wildfire, of people being taken, of disappearances, of bodies found in alleyways and market streets.

It wasn't just the city. It felt as though all of East Pakistan was burning.

One evening, sat watching television, as Abbi always did.

He was scolding us gently, frustrated that the children wouldn't go to bed on time. We giggled and lingered, trying to stretch the day just a little longer.

Then, suddenly, the news bulletin interrupted the usual programming.

War had begun.

Abbi froze. In an instant, he switched off the television and turned on the radio. Crackling through the static came the unmistakable voice of Indira Gandhi herself, declaring that war had broken out with Pakistan.

A terrible stillness filled the room. None of us knew what hour it was, only that the world had changed in a single breath. Then, without warning, the entire city went dark.

I heard Abbi's tense voice in the gloom. The war has started. It's a blackout.

Moments later, the wail of sirens echoed across the city, sharp, shrill, terrifying. Even now, that sound still pierces my memory like a blade.

At the first blast of the sirens, we rushed downstairs to Khala's portion of the house. All the children, Khala's and us, were gathered into one room and made to lie flat on our stomachs.

The adults hurried to cover the windows and doors with heavy sheets so that even the faintest glow from the candles wouldn't be seen from outside.

The next morning, as the grey light of dawn broke over the city, the sirens wailed once again.

Their sharp cry sliced through the uneasy calm.

It meant only one thing; another fighter plane was approaching.

Panic swept the streets. People ran wildly, searching for any shelter they could find.

Under our staircase was a large space. Abbi quickly gathered us there. He told Ammi, Nani, and all of us to sit quietly beneath the stairs, as low to the ground as we could.

Then, without a word, he scooped up my two little brothers, one in each arm, and sat under a tree nearby, shielding them with his own body.

We children couldn't understand.

Why would anyone want to drop bombs on us? Why would anyone want to kill us?

We had done nothing. We were just a family trying to live.

But the fighter planes didn't care about reasons.

Once again, the sky roared with the sound of engines, and the ground shook as bombs fell. This time, the airport suffered heavy damage.

That night passed with a little calmer. For the first time in days, everyone managed a bit of sleep.

By morning, life in the city seemed almost normal. Some shops reopened, and people ventured out to buy daily necessities.

Even we children, despite the fear of the past days, began to feel the pull of ordinary cravings. Semi Appa (Samina), always the more mischievous of us, whispered that she was longing for *jalebi*.

She and I were very close, partners in every little adventure.

At that moment, Abbi was bathing and Ammi was busy in the kitchen.

Quietly, without a word, Semi Appa and I slipped into the room, opened a drawer, and took out a few coins.

We hurried out into the street, heading toward the nearby alley where the jalebi shop stood.

As I was just handing over the money for the warm, sweet jalebis, the air was suddenly split by the sharp, chilling wail of the sirens.

Panic surged through us.

Semi Apa and I turned and sprinted toward home. But before we could reach our street, the roar of approaching fighter planes filled the sky.

We darted into the nearest house's garage, crouching behind a pile of crates.

As the planes roared overhead, we peeked out.

Through the noise and dust, we saw a figure running wildly down the road, our Abbi.

He was calling out our names, his voice desperate above the sounds of the sirens and engines.

We shouted back. His eyes found us instantly. Without a second thought for his safety, he ran toward us, arms outstretched.

When he reached us, he pulled us both into a fierce embrace, holding us so tightly it seemed he would never let go.

That moment, the fear, the relief, the overwhelming love, is etched in my memory even now.

Parents are the truest shelter, the mercy that shields us from the storms of the world.

At that moment, Abbi thought nothing of the danger.

He scolded us, then hugged us, then scolded us again. The emotions tumbled out so fast that, as children, we couldn't make sense of them.

But now, as a mother myself, I finally understand. I understand how a parent's heart aches for their children. How it breaks, how it loves, how it fears.

That evening, just as the day's fear had begun to settle, another incident shattered the fragile calm.

A plane, flames trailing from its body, crashed near the Town Hall.

We stood frozen as we watched the pilot eject, a white parachute blooming against the darkening sky. Everyone in the neighbourhood saw it.

Within moments, people surged toward the crash site.

We, too, ran with them, Abbi leading the way, holding our hands tightly.

The crowd buzzed with angry voices. People shouted, pointing toward where the plane had fallen.

Abbi kept asking, where did it crash? Where did it go down?

As we ran, I found myself thinking only of the pilot. He must be hurt badly. How terrible to fall from such a height.

When we reached the area, debris from the aircraft lay scattered across the ground. People were already picking up pieces, souvenirs of the wreckage.

A short distance away, a large crowd had gathered. Shouts rose above the clamour, Maro! Maro! (beat him! beat him!)

It was the first truly horrifying moment of my young life.

Through the gaps in the crowd, I saw a man being beaten. Beaten by other men.

The same man we had seen drifting down from the sky had tried to hide in a nearby school building. But the crowd had found him.

They dragged him out and set upon him in fury.

Abbi immediately pushed us back.

Move away! Move away from here! he urged, his voice tense with fear.

The crowd was thick. It was hard to break free.

As he shielded us, he called out desperately to the mob, Stop!

He's a human being. The children are watching. Don't do this! But no one listened.

Somehow, Abbi managed to pull us away and forced a path through the crowd.

We stumbled back toward the safety of our home, the terrible sounds of violence still ringing in our ears.

It was a scene I would never forget. The first time I saw what happens when fear and anger consume humanity.

As soon as we reached home, Ammi was waiting at the door, her face tense with worry.

What were you thinking? she demanded. Why did you take Nadeem and Rosy (Rozina) into that chaos? Something could have happened to all of you!

Abbi sighed, rubbing a hand over his tired face. I didn't even realize the children had followed me. The pilot from the crashed plane they caught him. The crowd was beating him.

Ammi's face softened into sorrow. She shook her head. Ya God, whose child, was he? Why is this war happening? How many have already died since 1947? And still, people can't stop fighting.

Abbi sat down heavily. I don't know what will happen. My heart feels sick after what I saw. May God have mercy on all of us.

He turned to Ammi. You should have kept a closer eye on the children. Who knows what effect all this will have on their hearts.

Then Abbi's tone grew heavier, his voice laced with frustration.

I can't understand people. In the middle of this war, this chaos, they are still celebrating strange victories instead of praying to God for peace.

Ammi nodded sadly. That's the curse of war and conflict. People kill those they don't even know. No friendship. No enmity. They kill because they believe if they don't, they'll be killed themselves.

But no one stops to ask *why* they're killing.

This is all for those people who sit comfortably in power, who never even ask if the people below them have eaten today, or who have sacrificed what for their ambitions.

Abbi leaned back, his expression dark and thoughtful. You're right. The people are like chaff caught with the grain, crushed alongside it.

Both the killers and the victims lose in the end.

The room fell silent, the weight of their words pressing down as the shadows deepened around us.

Outside, the city braced for whatever would come next. Inside, we were beginning to understand a terrible truth, that in war, no one is truly safe.

After that terrible day, my parents returned to their daily routines, unaware that the horrifying scene we had witnessed had taken root deep within my young mind.

To them, life had to carry on, but for me, the memory of that brutal moment became a haunting dream, a shadow that crept into my thoughts and wrapped itself around my spirit.

They say we forget the joys of childhood, but we never forget its traumas.

That night, when I lay down to sleep, the same dreadful scene replayed again and again in my dreams. I would wake up frightened, my heart racing.

Each time, my Nani gathered me into her arms, whispering gentle stories to distract me, to ease the fear.

Even as a child, I had always been sensitive. I still am.

For the first time in my life, I had seen with my own eyes how anger could make people lose themselves entirely.

I had witnessed how hatred consumed reason and devoured the very humanity that people claimed to cherish.

In those moments of rage, all the lessons of compassion and kindness were forgotten.

The mind held only one thought hatred, fury, and vengeance.

And though I was just a child, something inside me understood a painful truth when people choose anger over understanding, they destroy not just others, but themselves.

Days blurred into weeks. we lost count of how much time had passed.

By now, we had become used to the sound of the sirens. That wailing cry, once terrifying, had become a grim part of daily life, a signal that yet another plane was coming to rain death upon us.

And we had grown accustomed to living in darkness. The blackouts, once frightening, now felt like a strange kind of safety.

Staying in the shadows had become a habit, almost a shield.

We no longer went anywhere. The streets that once rang with children's laughter were now silent.

Whenever fear grew too heavy, whenever the shadows seemed too deep, we would gather near our Nani.

Sensing our anxiety, she would pull us close and tell stories, not of war, but of her childhood.

She spoke of a small village in Bihar called "Mai", where she had grown up.

Her stories transported us to a time of fields and festivals, of simple joys and peaceful days.

But even as she told them, there was always sadness in her eyes.

She often cursed the day when, at the urging of our Phupphi, the family had left for East Pakistan.

She would sigh and say, why did we ever leave? Why did we ever believe a better life waited for us here?

Her heart remained forever tied to the memories of "Mai" and to her marital home, Sabzi Bagh's Ismail Manzil. She never forgot India.

She never forgot the home she had left behind.

While the world outside seemed to fall apart, Nani's memories became a refuge for us.

A fading link to a peaceful past that now seemed impossibly far away.

We no longer saw Mohan's Mamoo.

There were no more visits to "Imli Wali Nani".

No more playing at Saba's house.

No more doll weddings.

The alleyways and courtyards that once echoed with laughter now stood silent, filled only with fear and shadows.

It was as if life itself had abandoned us.

Each night, the only sound that broke the stillness was Mohan's Mamoo's voice.

Somewhere, his window would creak open.

Then, into the silent darkness, he would shout his strange, upside-down chant

"Takbeer. Nara-e-Allah-o-Akbar!"

But there was no victorious cry. His tone was twisted, trembling, almost mocking in its fear.

As soon as the words rang out, the window would slam shut again.

The younger children giggled nervously, not fully understanding.

But the adults would only glance toward the sound, eyes heavy with sadness.

Perhaps Mamoo had gone half-mad. Or maybe it was his way of coping with the terror that gripped us all. He had always been a gentle, innocent man.

Days passed fifteen, twenty, we lost track. Then, suddenly, Dhaka fell.

The brief war came to a crushing end. The Pakistan Army surrendered.

I do not recall the exact date, but history tells me it was December 16, 1971.

Never before had the world witnessed a defeat like this.

General A. K. Niazi, standing not only before the Indian Army but before the eyes of the world, handed over his pistol and with it, he surrendered half a nation.

After that, the Indian Army and the Mukti Bahini began entering the city.

The streets that had once been divided by uneasy alliances now became pathways of conquest.

When love or loyalty breaks, whether between people or nations, the storm that follows is always devastating.

We felt that storm now. We had embraced this land as our own.

And yet, destiny had already written another journey for us.

The life of wanderers. Of those who would never again be sure where they truly belonged.

****

CIVIL WAR

What happens to a city after a war. May no soul ever witness it. As terrifying as war is, civil war is far worse.

In a battle, destruction strikes once, a bomb falls, lives are lost, and it's over.

But in a civil war, you die slowly, piece by piece. You never know when or where betrayal will come.

Who will be a friend? Who will be the foe? Who will offer shelter? And who will leave you exposed and defenceless?

After the fall of Dhaka, as Mukti Bahini fighters began to pour into the city, fear seeped into every home. Anxiety became a constant, unwanted guest.

The non-Bengalis, especially those who had migrated from India years ago, now began to feel the ground shifting beneath their feet.

They no longer trusted the walls of their own homes.

Many families, gripped by fear, abandoned their houses, moving from one hiding place to another.

Some began desperately searching for a way to flee the country altogether. Panic rippled through the streets.

Neighbours who once shared food and laughter began to whisper not in friendship, but in fear. Some betrayed each other just to save their own lives. Others pointed fingers to claim property or to loot in the chaos.

It seemed that people had become refugees within their own homes. Those seeking shelter were finding themselves stripped of it.

In the quest for safety, people became more lost than ever before.

Next to our old house, as I had mentioned before, was a home belonging to a Bengali family.

When the troubles had first begun, even before the war, they had wisely left the city and disappeared.

During their absence, the relatives living below us had broken down a section of the shared wall, claiming it was to access water. No one thought much of it at the time.

But now, after the fall of Dhaka, the Bengali family returned. And when they saw their broken wall, they flew into a rage.

By then, during all the turmoil, Ammi and Abbi had already made the painful decision to abandon our beloved house in Mohammadpur.

We had taken refuge in a vacant home in another neighbourhood. We thought we had left the danger behind. But the past has a way of following you.

When the angry neighbours discovered the damage to their property, our helpful relatives, desperate to save themselves, did the unthinkable.

They blamed Abbi.

Now, that neighbours weren't just angry. He was looking for Abbi.

The boy who had lived with us, Abdul, the same loyal child we had left to watch over the Mohammadpur house, became our eyes and ears.

He would come running at odd hours to warn us about the neighbourhood's shifting dangers.

That day, his face was pale with urgency.

Baba, he whispered, don't come back here. The family next door has returned. They've seen the broken wall. They're saying it was you who did it. They're searching for you.

This was Abbi's second harsh lesson in the school of survival.
Never place your trust in anyone, especially in hard times. And it was true.

It was in these dark days that we began to see the real faces behind familiar masks.

War had become the great teacher of human nature. It taught us who was truly a friend. And who would turn into an enemy when the world began to fall apart?

We had only been living in the new neighbourhood for three days.

One morning, around six o'clock, Abbi stepped out to observe the surroundings, to feel the pulse of this unfamiliar place.

But as the morning stretched on, the hours crept past.

By nine o'clock, he still hadn't returned. Ammi and Nani's worry began to bloom into fear.

Ammi kept going to the door, stepping outside, scanning the quiet streets, and returning inside each time more anxious than the last.

Soon, she was in tears. She didn't know what to do.

Nani, always the voice of wisdom even in the worst times, finally spoke.

Go outside and ask the neighbours. Maybe someone has seen him.

Ammi wiped her eyes, gathered her courage, and stepped out into the unfamiliar streets. She didn't know anyone here.

Still, she stopped every passerby, asking softly, urgently, if they had seen her husband. But no one had answers. Exhausted and heartbroken, she returned home.

Nani thought for a moment, then made a decision.

Let's go back to the old house. Maybe Abdul knows something. By now, it was nearly 12:30 P.M.

Ammi, Nani, and all of us children gathered ourselves and made the difficult journey back to Mohammadpur.

The streets felt heavier than before, weighted down by the unknown.

At around one o'clock, our cousin came rushing upstairs.

Her face was pale, her words trembling.

Khala, before you arrived, we were up on the rooftop. We saw soldiers taking Khalu away in a truck.

The ground seemed to shift beneath us. The nightmare we had feared had become real.

Abbi had been taken.

At those words, it was as if Ammi's soul left her body. She collapsed where she stood, unconscious.

Nani was frozen in shock, not knowing what to do. We children burst into tears.

Abdul tried to calm us, his small hands patting our backs while glancing helplessly at Ammi.

Nani hurried to splash water on Ammi's face, calling her name again and again.

Finally, Ammi stirred, her eyes fluttering open.

Before she could speak, Abdul leaned in, urgency in his voice.

Maa, why did you come back here? The neighbour, one next door, he's joined the Mukti Bahini now. He's still looking for Baba because of the wall. He's gone out somewhere now, but he could return any moment.

And Baba's Foxy car, he took it. Only the van is still outside.

You must leave. Quickly.

But Ammi was in no state to go anywhere. She clutched her chest, tears streaming down her face. Hours seemed to stretch painfully.

At around 2:30 P.M., when Ammi had regained some strength, Nani urged her gently, Let's go. We must leave before it's too late.

But just as we gathered ourselves, we heard footsteps on the stairs. All of us froze.

Then, suddenly, we saw Abbi climbing up toward us.

Our fear shattered into sheer joy. We screamed, Abbi's back! Abbi's back!

Ammi, as though touched by some hidden strength, ran toward him.

Abbi gathered all of us into his arms and began to weep, not tears of sorrow, but of overwhelming relief.

My Najma, he whispered, offer nafil prayers. Whatever good deed we've done must have spoken for us today. God has granted me a new life.

He turned to Nani, voice still shaking, Amma, keep praying for us as you always have.

When the first rush of emotions settled, Ammi asked quietly, where did you go? What happened to you?

Before Abbi could answer, Abdul rushed back.

The neighbours have left for a day, he said breathlessly. I heard it from their servant. You must leave by this evening.

Abbi nodded.

Abdul, he said, start gathering whatever essentials we have.

As Abdul ran to do as he was told, Ammi turned again to Abbi.

Tell us, she pleaded. Where were you? What happened?

Abbi took a deep breath.

And then, with the weight of all he had seen, he began to tell us everything.

Abbi began to speak, his voice low and steady, though the memory weighed heavily on him.

When I stepped out this morning, I noticed a Mukti Bahini patrol passing by.

At first, fear seized me. But then I thought, if I turned and ran, it would only draw suspicion.

So, I kept walking casually, trying to appear unbothered.

That was my mistake.

Suddenly, the Mukti Bahini vehicle screeched to a stop.

One of the men jumped out and grabbed Abbi by the arm.

Who are you? How many Bengalis have you killed? You look like a Razakar spy to me.'

Another shouted, no, this one seems like their leader. Take him with us!

Abbi tried to explain, you're mistaken. I've done nothing.

But they wouldn't listen.

They shoved him roughly into their jeep and drove off toward an unknown destination.

As the city streets flashed by, Abbi's thoughts turned only to us.

What will happen now?

Ya God, my wife and children, they have no protector but You. You alone are our Helper.

The jeep stopped outside a house. But it wasn't a home.

It was one of the Mukti Bahini's secret detention sites.

They dragged Abbi inside and locked him in a room.

Inside that room were forty other prisoners.

How many more were locked away in other rooms, Abbi could not imagine.

The doors were not wooden, they were iron-barred gates, like those in a prison.

Abbi was forced to stand by the gate there was no room to sit.

As his eyes adjusted to the dim light, he saw that the walls and floor were stained with blood.

The other prisoners' eyes reflected the same fear that gripped his own heart.

Beside him stood an elderly man, so old he might have died of natural causes in a matter of days. Yet, here he was, dragged into this nightmare.

Next to the old man stood a boy, no older than fourteen.

Abbi's heart clenched. He recognized the boy. He was the son of Jamali Sahib, one of our neighbours. A kind, gentle child.

What crime had he committed to deserve this?

Abbi realized then that death was hovering over them all.

If there was any hope left, it was not in the hands of men.

Only God's mercy could save them now.

As he stood there, Abbi's mind reeled with a terrible thought.

All of us were Muslims. yet we had become enemies to one another. Brothers turning against brothers. And for what?

For language. For land.

For things that could never justify the killing of fellow believers.

The men who had captured Abbi at 6 A.M had already left.

A new group of Mukti Bahini guards had taken over.

By noon, the next shift would come.

But the men who had arrested Abbi were due to return at 4 P.M

And it was they who would decide his fate.

Abbi, ever a smoker, always carried two packs of expensive cigarettes in his pocket.

That morning, by sheer chance, one pack was half empty and the other untouched.

He also wore his Rolex watch, a treasured gift from a friend. Even now, it gleamed on his wrist, its ticking hands counting down the uncertain hours.

In the suffocating room, standing amid fear and dried blood, Abbi pulled a cigarette from his pack, lit it with his lighter, and took a deep drag.

He rested his hand, the one wearing the Rolex, on the iron-barred door.

The guard watching the prisoners began to glance at him.

Once.

Twice.

Then again.

He would walk toward Abbi, then turn back, as though struggling with some thought.

Finally, the guard approached fully.

Give me a cigarette.

Abbi silently handed him one.

The man took it eagerly, lit it, inhaled.

Then, after a pause, he said with chilling bluntness, Why hold back? You won't be needing them after four o'clock. Give me the whole pack.

Abbi steadied his voice.

I'll give you the whole pack. But tell me, why have we been imprisoned? What is our crime?

It took courage to even ask.

The guard leaned closer, voice low and cold.

The commanders will be back at four. They will kill all of you. That's what this place is for. You people, you're our enemies.

Abbi swallowed the rising fear and tried to reason with him.

We don't even know each other. How can we be enemies?

If you help me, I'll pray for you for the rest of my life. My wife and children have no one else.

For God's sake, fear God.

We share the same faith. Do something good. Earn a little mercy in the eyes of the Almighty.

In that desperate moment, Abbi placed all his hope in the fragile thread of shared humanity.

And in the heart of a stranger who held his life in his hands.

The guard stared at Abbi for a long moment.

Silence stretched between them.

Then he spoke.

Alright. I will help you escape. But I want your watch.

Abbi nodded without hesitation. Take it. The watch is yours.

The guard's eyes flicked toward the other men in the room.

Be ready. When the duty changes at noon, I will get you out.

At those words, the elderly man standing beside Abbi clasped his hands together in silent pleading.

The boy, the son of Jamali Sahib, began to weep.

Uncle, please, he sobbed. Please save me too.

Abbi's heart twisted at the sound. He turned back to the guard.

Listen, Abbi said softly, urgently. I'm already giving you a very expensive watch and a full pack of cigarettes.

Do me one more kindness. Let these two go with me.

That old man, he will pass away on his own in a few days. Why carry the burden of his blood?

And this poor boy, he has not even begun his life yet.

If you are taking such a risk for me, take it for them as well. Let them go.

The guard hesitated.

It's dangerous for me too, he muttered.

But after a pause, he nodded.

Alright. I will release them with you.

But no more. Don't ask me for anyone else.

Now sit quietly. Don't say a word.

I'll go check the situation outside.

Abbi exhaled slowly, barely able to believe what was happening.

Hope, so small and fragile, flickered to life in the darkness.

And once again, it wasn't bullets or power that would decide their fate.

It was the rare and precious mercy of a single human heart.

Once the guard stepped away, a quiet murmur filled the crowded room.

One by one, the other prisoners began turning toward Abbi.

Their eyes, filled with a fragile blend of hope and despair, pleaded silently for help.

Some whispered desperate requests, believing Abbi might be their savior too.

But Abbi's heart sank.

How could he save anyone else when he was fighting for his own life?

His own fate hung by a single, fraying thread.

He didn't know what would become of these men.

Each face watched him with longing, as though willing him to take them along.

Abbi could not meet their eyes.

The weight of their hope was unbearable.

Then, the guard returned.

Without wasting a second, he spoke quickly.

Listen. At exactly quarter to twelve, our shift will begin to change. I'll release you three at that time.

It's eleven now.

When I open the door, head right. Don't look left or right.

Keep walking straight until you're out the gate.

Then run as far and as fast as you can.

From there, your fate is your own.

If you're caught, I won't be responsible.

Now, he added, give me the watch and the pack of cigarettes.

Abbi nodded.

Alright, brother. We'll do as you say.

Beyond this, our lives are in God's hands. Life and death belong only to Him.

Abbi handed over the Rolex watch and the full cigarette pack.

But even as he did, doubt gnawed at him.

What if the guard was lying? What if, now that he had the watch and cigarettes, he would change his mind?

Time seemed to slow to a crawl. Every second felt like an hour.

Abbi could hear nothing but the pounding of his own heart.

Finally, as the clock edged toward, at **11:45**, the guards began leaving their posts.

The shift was changing.

The guard returned, his eyes darting nervously around the room.

Come on, he whispered urgently. Hurry. Move fast.

The gate will open soon, and new guards will take over. They won't know who you are.

When I tell you, slip out and don't stop.

Freedom was so close. And yet, so perilous.

The guard slid open the door. Go. Now.

Abbi, the elderly man, and the young boy quickly stepped forward. Abbi cast one last glance over his shoulder.

The remaining prisoners stood frozen, their eyes full of desperate, silent pleas.

Abbi felt as though their stares pierced through his very soul.

He could barely bear it. But he had no choice.

With a heavy heart, he turned away and hurried forward.

The three slipped through the iron gate without looking left or right.

At that moment, a jeep carrying the new guards was pulling in through the entrance. But no one stopped them.

They crossed the threshold between captivity and freedom, though danger still lurked on every side.

Once outside, they kept walking swiftly, forcing themselves to remain calm.

When they were a safe distance away, they broke into a run.

They didn't stop until they reached the mosque near Mohammadpur.

There, breathless and shaken, they each offered two rakats of nafil shukrana, prayers of gratitude.

God had delivered them from the slaughterhouse.

Afterward, they agreed it was safest to part ways.

The old man, the boy, and Abbi each disappeared into the uncertain streets of Dhaka, bound by fate and faith.

Abbi decided to first return to the old house.

As he crossed the road, he noticed groups of Mukti Bahini moving through the area but Indian Army soldiers were also nearby.

Abbi had observed that when the Indian Army was present, the Mukti Bahini did not harass or seize Urdu-speaking civilians.

The Indian Army seemed to understand the fragile, dangerous atmosphere of civil unrest.

Suddenly, a vehicle from the Indian Army pulled up sharply in front of Abbi. His heart sank.

Out of the frying pan, into the fire, he thought grimly.

Now what?

A soldier gestured to him.

Come here. Where do you live?

Abbi answered carefully.

Here in Mohammadpur.

The soldier leaned closer.

Tell me, He said, do you know where the Town Planner's house is?

(Here, it's worth mentioning, in any war, the **Town Planner** becomes a crucial figure. He knows every road, every alley of the city.)

Abbi nodded nervously.

Yes, sir. I know it.

But his heart was racing. His thoughts were not with the Army or the city's roads.

They were with Ammi and children. He needed to get home.

The soldier gave a small smile.

Take us there. Don't be afraid, we won't harm you.

Abbi had no choice.

Yes, sir. I'll show you.

He climbed into the jeep.

(This was the exact moment when my cousin, watching from the rooftop, had seen him being taken away by the Indian Army.)

The jeep sped through the uneasy streets of Dhaka. Soon, they arrived at the Town Planner's house.

Abbi stepped out and knocked on the door.

From inside came a cautious voice.

Who is it?

Khalu (khala Husband), Abbi replied. It's me, Shamim.

The Indian Army officer turned to Abbi.

Do you know him?

Yes, Abbi replied. He's my relative my khala's husband.

At that moment, the door creaked open.

Before anyone could react, the Indian soldiers swiftly moved past Abbi and entered the house.

Abbi's fate was once again hanging by a thread.

As soon as the door opened, Khalu looked at the uniformed soldiers, alarm flashing in her eyes.

Who are you people? What do you want? Shamim, why have you brought them here?!

Abbi raised his hands helplessly.

Khalu, I don't know. I've been caught in trouble since this morning. One disaster barely ends before another begins.

The Indian officer stepped forward, calm but firm.

Please, don't be afraid. We mean you no harm.

We only need a detailed map of Dhaka.

Right now, there are small incidents happening, but soon this will turn into full-scale civil war.

We need to understand the city's layout and key areas.

If you help us, we'll provide you with Army protection.

Khalu, the Town Planner, nodded. Come with me.

He led the soldiers to his home office.

There, he explained which areas were sensitive and dangerous.

He then handed over a full map of the city, complete with his professional notes and markings.

When the soldiers had gathered all the information they needed, Abbi finally spoke.

Sir, could you please drop me back at Mohammadpur?

The streets are dangerous for me now.

The men who arrested me this morning might still be searching.

The officer nodded.

Alright. We'll drop you at Mohammadpur.

If you want, we can even bring your family there for safety.

Abbi shook his head gently.

Just take me there.

If my family has returned to the old house, I'll find them.

If they're not there, you can leave.

Abbi paused, glancing around at all of us as he finished recounting his incredible journey.

And just now, he said softly, the Indian Army dropped me here.

It was Abdul downstairs who told me you were all in this house.

At that, Ammi covered her face and wept.

We clung to Abbi, relief and gratitude flooding the room.

For now, the family was whole again.

And somehow, despite everything, God had brought Abbi back to us.

After hearing Abbi's harrowing story, both Ammi and Nani seemed frozen in shock.

For a long moment, neither spoke.

Then, as if remembering what truly mattered, they quietly spread their prayer mats and offered two rakats of nafil shukrana, giving thanks for Abbi's miraculous return.

When the prayers ended, Ammi gathered herself and told Abbi, Abdul has warned us. He says we shouldn't stay here any longer.

Abbi immediately called Abdul and asked him to explain everything he knew.

Abdul, ever loyal, told Abbi about the mounting danger, the neighbour still searching, Mukti Bahini patrols nearby, and rumour's spreading in the area.

Abbi listened carefully, his expression growing grave.

That settles it, he said at last. We can't stay here another minute. He turned to Ammi.

We're going to Khalu's house (Town planner). The Indian Army has stationed protection there.

Gather only the essential things. We must leave immediately.

Ammi nodded, wiping her tears.

There was no time to waste.

Once again, they would leave behind a home filled with memories, heading into the unknown.

But this time, they carried something far greater than belongings,

The hope of survival and the blessing of family unity.

Ammi and Nani moved swiftly, their hands trembling but determined.

They gathered three or four sets of clothes for everyone.

Nani carefully packed her jewellery, while Ammi grabbed powdered milk tins for the children, a few food supplies, and whatever cash they had left.

Abbi collected all his important papers and documents, stacking them in neat bundles. Everything was loaded into the van. Abbi turned to Abdul.

What about the other vehicle?

Abdul lowered his gaze.

The Mukti Bahini took it. They drove it away.

Abbi's face tightened, but there was no time for anger or sorrow. Then pack the rest of the things into this van.

Without wasting a second, Abdul began loading the remaining belongings.

He tied the family's chickens and placed them carefully into the van's storage area.

He gathered whatever vegetables he could find and added them as well. Soon, everything was ready.

We all climbed into the van. As Abdul moved to get in, Abbi placed a firm hand on his shoulder.

No, Abdul. You won't come with us.

Abdul's eyes widened.

But, Baba

Abbi shook his head.

You'll stay here.

Keep living in this house.

And most importantly, keep bringing us news about what's happening.

We need you now more than ever.

Abdul swallowed his protest and nodded.

Even at his young age, he understood the weight of the responsibility being placed upon him.

The doors closed. The engine roared to life.

And once again, our family was on the move, leaving behind another home, stepping into the unknown, held together by faith, resilience, and the hope of finding refuge.

As soon as Abbi started the engine, we children, cried out at once.

Abdul will come with us! Why can't he?!

Abbi sighed deeply.

He cannot come. Abdul is Bengali.

If we take him with us, people might think we've kidnapped him.

If someone stops us along the road, it will put not only our lives but Abdul's life in danger too.

Ammi's eyes filled with tears.

But I've raised this child for years. He has no one else. Where will he go?

Abdul, who had stood silently all this time, finally spoke in a trembling voice.

Amma, take me with you.

I cannot live without you. I can't stay alone.

Ammi turned to Abbi, her voice pleading.

Please; for my sake, take him with us.

Abbi shook his head, his face tense.

Why don't you understand?

If we take Abdul, someone might think we've captured a Bengali child. The streets are dangerous.

If he comes with us, it will endanger not only us but him too.

Abbi looked at Abdul with sorrow.

Son, forgive us.

Then, without another word, he pressed the accelerator.

The van lurched forward.

Tears streamed down all our faces.

Even Abbi's eyes glistened.

As the van picked up speed, Abdul began running after us.

Amma, don't leave me! Don't go without me!

His voice rang out, breaking our hearts.

He ran behind the van for what felt like miles, his small figure growing smaller and smaller in the distance.

Until he finally disappeared from view.

We sobbed as we drove away, leaving behind not just a house, but Abdul, who was more than a servant, more than a helper. He had been family.

To this day, we don't know where he is. Whether he survived or not or he is still alive, but we never forget him.

We finally arrived at Khalu's house, seeking refuge, we were not alone.

Inside, forty-five men, women, and children had gathered, families of doctors, engineers, and businessmen.

In times of war, it is always the professionals and tradespeople who face the greatest dangers. Their skills and wealth make them target.

Because of Khalu's position, and the importance of the families sheltering there, the Indian Army had stationed guards outside the house. For now, it was a fragile bubble of safety in a collapsing world.

The food supplies we had brought with us from home began to dwindle.

Worse still were the cries of Nazia and Rehan, my two youngest siblings.

They were still infants, just a year apart in age, both dependent on milk.

But their milk tins were nearly empty, and so was the little money we had left.

Hunger made them cry and with every wail, fair gripped us tighter. What if the Mukti Bahini heard them?

What if they stormed the house, thinking we were hiding something. The lives of forty-five people hung in the balance with every sob.

We were forced to cover the babies' mouths gently when they cried, muffling their voices to prevent the sound from escaping the house.

At night, Rehan slept in Ammi's arms, Nazia in Nani's.

Sometimes, they were taken into a separate room and the door shut tight, in the desperate hope that no sound would carry outside. The house was full of people.

But silence ruled over us like a heavy, suffocating blanket. And in that silence, we lived day to day, praying that somehow, we would all survive.

One morning, Abbi turned to Ammi with a grave expression.

Najma, he said quietly, I need you to take one of the children and go to the bank. Try to withdraw some money.

The situation in the city is getting worse. I can't risk going out myself.

We're all in danger, but for you, it may be slightly less.

Ammi nodded.

Alright. Just sign the cheques and tell me what to do when I get there.

Abbi carefully wrote out several cheques and handed them to her.

Ammi gathered the papers and took Nadeem by the hand.

Then, heart pounding, she stepped out into the tense, silent streets.

The whole city seemed wrapped in fear. Shops were shuttered. People moved quickly and spoke in hushed tones. At last, Ammi reached the bank.

Inside, only Bengali-speaking staff were present. No one was speaking Urdu.

Still, she gathered her courage and walked to the counter.

Years of living in Bengal had made both Abbi and Ammi fluent in Bengali.

Brother, she said politely, please cash this cheque quickly. My child is restless and the children at home are hungry.

The clerk glanced at her and frowned.

Your cheque cannot be cashed. All accounts have been frozen.

Ammi's heart sank.

But this is my money! How can you keep it? Will we starve while you hold our savings?

The man shook his head. I can't help you. If you don't understand, speak to the manager. He's over there.

Ammi gathered Nadeem close and approached the man he had pointed to.

Brother, please. I have some money in my account. Kindly allow me to withdraw it. The clerk says the account is closed.

The manager leaned back in his chair.

Yes, the accounts are closed, but I can help you, if you agree to my terms.

What terms? Ammi asked warily.

For every thousand takas, we will give you eight hundred. We'll keep two hundred as our fee, and you can only withdraw up to one thousand takas.

Ammi paused, her mind racing, it was unjust, it was robbery but the children were hungry. There was no choice.

Fine, she whispered. Give me whatever you can.

The manager handed over eight hundred takas, keeping two hundred for himself.

Ammi clutched the money tightly, took Nadeem's hand, and hurried home.

Her thoughts spun with worry. What will we do next? How long can we survive like this.

Back at the house, she explained everything to Abbi.

We can't get our money now, she finished softly. All the accounts are closed.

Abbi sighed. This too is a test. God is still with us.

Nani nodded in agreement, her face calm in the storm. Leave everything to God, my child. He has protected us so far. Life and death are in His hands.

And once again, faith was the only wealth we could still count on.

While the adults battled fear and uncertainty, we children lived in our innocent world, unaware of the full weight of the dangers that surrounded us.

The house where we had taken refuge stood next to another home. Its boundary wall had either crumbled or been broken down.

One day, while playing, Nadeem and I slipped through the gap.

The house beyond was large and beautiful, though it now stood eerily silent.

Not a single soul seemed to be inside. As we wandered further, we spotted six golf balls lying scattered on the floor.

Delighted by the discovery, we scooped them up and continued exploring.

But as we pushed open the door to the next room, our excitement froze.

Inside, we saw several people lying motionless on the floor.

At first, our young minds did not understand. We moved closer, curiosity overcoming caution. By the doorway stood a large cabinet and from behind its door, a human hand protruded, stiff and stained with dried blood. We crept forward, hearts pounding.

Just then, Abbi burst into the room.

Before we could even react, he grabbed both of us and whisked us away.

As he hurried us back, we heard him telling Ammi, his voice tight with worry,

Keep a closer watch on the children. They slipped into the house next door.

There were bodies inside. Thanks God I arrived in time.

Otherwise, they would have been terrified out of their minds

We didn't fully understand what we had seen that day. But something changed within us. Even childhood had begun to lose its innocence.

As long as the Indian Army remained in our neighbourhood, there was a fragile sense of peace.

But as soon as they withdrew, the Mukti Bahini swept in like a storm

They began raiding homes, looting, and spreading terror.

The same chaos consumed our old neighbourhood, Mohammadpur.

The Mukti Bahini patrolled every alley and street, searching, threatening, taking what they wanted.

One day, despite her fear, Ammi decided to risk a journey back to the old neighbourhood to collect a few necessities.

As she approached the familiar gates, her eyes fell upon a small, familiar figure.

Abdul.

The moment he spotted her, he ran up, breathless.

Amma! Others have taken shelter in the house!

Ammi followed him upstairs.

There, she found Molvi Sahib and his family huddled together, seeking refuge in the home we had once called ours.

Ammi asked after their well-being, offering whatever comfort she could.

Then, gathering a few clothes, she prepared to leave. But Abdul clung to her side.

Amma, at least show me where you are staying now. I'll come ahead and deliver the things. It's dangerous for you.

Ammi hesitated, then nodded.

Alright. Let's go.

Together, they made their way back to the house where we were now staying.

Abdul's eyes widened as he took in the unfamiliar surroundings, the crowd of anxious faces, the lingering air of fear.

Abbi immediately called him aside. Tell me, Abdul, how are the people in the old neighbourhood faring?

The room fell silent, everyone waiting for the boy's news. And what Abdul shared next would weigh heavily on all our hearts.

Abdul stood solemnly before Abbi; his face older than his years.

Sahib, after you left, the Mukti Bahini came to the house, he began.

They asked who I was.

I told them I had no family. That I was just hiding in the empty house.

They asked where the owners had gone.

I told them I didn't know.

Abbi listened, eyes narrowed, bracing himself.

They also went to Mohun's house, Abdul continued. But those people had fled the night before.

The Mukti Bahini stormed Imli Wali Nani's house too. I don't know if they escaped or were killed. I haven't seen them since.

He hesitated. His gaze drifted toward us children. Abbi noticed and gently led Abdul aside, away from our ears.

Tell me the rest, he urged

Years later, when I began writing this book, Abbi told me what Abdul had whispered that day

When the Mukti Bahini reached Saba's house, the grand house where the famous doll's wedding once filled the streets with joy, they dragged everyone out. The men were beaten and killed.

The women, including Saba, fled to the rooftop.

When the Mukti Bahini came for them, the women, holding each other tight, leapt from the roof. Every single one including Saba. No one Survived.

Who could have imagined?

That the same girl whose doll's wedding had once made the whole neighbourhood dance with delight, would meet such a terrible end?

A child, raised like a delicate flower, now broken on the stones below.

Abdul's voice had quivered as he recounted the horror.

In Mohammadpur, almost everyone was either killed or fled, like us.

And many who tried to escape didn't even make it to safety.

Abbi closed his eyes, grief washing over him.

Only those whom God chose to spare survived.

And so, yet again, we understood, in war, no memory remains sacred.

No childhood remains untouched.

And survival is the rarest miracle of all.

Even those who tried to escape, Abdul had said, many were cut down along the way.

The Mukti Bahini had developed a new, terrifying habit, they would burst into any house, anytime, taking whatever they pleased. Cars. Clothes. Jewellery. Food.

Nothing was off-limits.

Ammi, always thinking ahead, had hidden what little food and valuables we still possessed inside a broken crate.

But Nani, wise and cautious, had taken an extra step.

Without telling anyone, she stitched the family's jewellery into a pillow.

Some smaller pieces, she tucked away into the empty spaces of milk tins.

In times of war, even gold had to be disguised as something ordinary.

For the day might come, and it seemed it soon would, when those hidden treasures would be the only hope for survival or bargaining.

Every corner of our lives was now a secret.

Every day, a gamble between being discovered or living another dawn.

That day, even the house where forty to forty-five of us had taken refuge was no longer safe. Without warning, the Mukti Bahini stormed in. They began looting whatever they could lay their hands on.

I watched as Nani, calm even in terror, pressed a pillow into Nazia's small hands.

It was her habit to wander around holding a pillow, but this time, Nani gave her two.

She closed the lid of the milk tin, handed it to Rehan, and gave Nadeem another item to play with.

Then she whispered for them to sit quietly in a corner and crouched beside them. We children didn't understand. Why was Nani always so protective of that pillow? Why did she insist the babies carry the milk tins?

Then, the raiders began interrogating each adult. Their voices were harsh.

Their hands were harsher. Beatings broke out amid the looting.

At that moment, Abbi lay quietly on a mat, dressed simply in a lungi and vest.

Others wore pajamas and kurtas, or pants and shirts.

The Mukti Bahini men questioned each person.

What do you do?

Those who admitted they were doctors or engineers were dragged aside and lined up against a wall.

When they came to Abbi, they barked, and you? What's your work?

Abbi answered in a steady voice,

I push a cart. I sell vegetables.

The men moved on.

They grabbed the engineer and doctor who had spoken honestly, and took them away.

In that moment, Nani's wisdom became clear.

The pillow Nazia clutched held the family's hidden jewellery.

The milk tins the boys held concealed what little wealth we had left.

She had turned the children into the safest vaults.

For who would search a child's toy or pillow when they were already stealing lives?

Two days earlier, Abbi had secretly sent Abdul to deliver a message to Rehman Uncle, pleading for help.

Now, barely half an hour after the Mukti Bahini's terrifying raid, Rehman Uncle arrived not alone, but with his two sons.

The very sons whose lives Abbi had once saved.

Rehman Uncle turned to them and said, do you recognize him?

Shamim Uncle. He saved your lives. Now, it's your turn to help him.

They nodded solemnly.

Abbi quickly explained what had just happened, how the Mukti Bahini had stormed the house, taken the engineer and the doctor, and left everyone in terror.

If you could help free them and move us to a safer place, it would be a great kindness.

But Rehman Uncle shook his head firmly. No. This is no kindness. It's the debt we owe.

They say everything happens for a reason.

God had made Abbi save Rehman's uncle's son that day because God knew we would need Rehman's uncle someday for help and survive. It was always part of God's plan.

Rehman Uncle turned to his sons.

Go. Find where they've taken the doctor and engineer. Bring them back if you can.

Once that's done, we'll arrange for everyone's safe passage out of here.

Before leaving, the two young men posted two Mukti Bahini guards outside the house to ensure no one disturbed us. Then they disappeared into the streets.

An hour later, they returned, and with them, the doctor and engineer, both shaken but alive.

They promised they would soon return with a plan to relocate everyone to safety.

At that moment, Rehman Uncle and his sons seemed nothing short of angels.

In that hour of desperation, one truth became clear. Good deeds are never lost.

They may vanish for a time, forgotten by people.

But when the darkest nights fall, God brings their reward back, often through the very hands you once helped.

Soon after, a Mukti Bahini soldier, sent by Rehman Uncle's sons, arrived and quietly handed out food to the families inside.

In the middle of a brutal war, amidst betrayal and hatred, a simple act of humanity stood like a shining beacon.

A Bengali man helping non-Bengalis because humanity has no language. No race. No boundary.

By now, all our money had run out.

Once again, Ammi took Nadeem by the hand and ventured back to the bank

But this time, the familiar faces were gone. Strangers sat behind the counters.

When Ammi pleaded for our money, they refused.

She returned home, heartbroken. All she had left were eight annas.

Word of our plight soon reached Dr. Manima Islam's parents, who were hiding with us. They quietly pressed 200 rupees into Ammi's hands.

Take this, they insisted gently. Buy something for the children.

Ammi hesitated. Her pride resisted. But for the sake of her little ones, she finally accepted.

(She later returned the money to them after the war, for Ammi's dignity was a treasure no hardship could steal.)

Yet life grew only more difficult. The greatest hardship was for our youngest siblings, still needing milk to survive. But crying could mean discovery. Death.

So, they were not allowed to weep aloud.

Little Rehan, once so lively, now lived in constant fear. His voice began to stammer.

He sobbed silently, trembling, afraid someone might cover his mouth to keep him quiet forever and Nazia, she no longer made a sound.

Her tears slipped silently down her cheeks. Her eyes, once wide with curiosity, were now clouded with fear. That was how war stole even a child's right to cry

Two days later, at dawn, Rehman Uncle and his sons returned.

They brought a jeep and an army truck.

It's time, Rehman Uncle announced. Gather your things quickly.

Everyone in the safehouse, all the families hiding together, scrambled to collect what little they had.

Among them were Abbi's distant aunt and uncle. His aunt had once been a school principal.

Nani packed two precious milk tins into a basket. She added a small bottle of milk and whatever bits of food she could find.

Then, as always, she handed Nazia and Rehan their two small pillows, more than comfort now, they were guardians of the family's remaining valuables.

Soon, everyone began climbing into the army truck.

But as Nani tried to lift the basket into the truck, Abbi's aunt snatched it away.

There isn't enough space for your basket, she said sharply, placing it back on the ground.

If we survive, we can always get more things later.

She never paused to think the basket held the only milk for the smallest children.

Just then, the soldiers began shouting.

The Mukti Bahini had been tipped off.

They were approaching. The truck engine roared to life. There was no time to argue. The basket and the milk were left behind.

I'll never forget what came next.

The Indian soldiers lifted Nadeem and me into their laps. We sat at the edge of the truck, trembling.

Semi Appa stayed near Ammi, while Nazia, Rehan, Nani, and Abbi sat inside with the others.

The truck was packed.

Behind us, a swarm of Mukti Bahini fighters burst onto the road. Spears. Swords. They were running fast too fast.

We began to cry, clutching the soldiers' uniforms.

The soldiers loaded their rifles, fingers ready on the triggers.

If they come closer, we shoot.

The truck lurched forward, racing down the road.

I don't remember how long they chased us. It felt like forever.

But at a sharp bend, the pursuers finally disappeared from view.

We gasped in relief. But our terror was far from over.

The truck and jeep drove us to the army cantonment area, stopping near the home of Tamanna Khan, an engineer and Rehman Uncle's relative.

Everyone out, the soldiers ordered.

Rehman Uncle gathered the adults.

From now on, no Urdu, he warned. Specially the women. If you speak, use Bengali and only when absolutely necessary. The servants could be informants.

Keep the children inside all times.

Tamanna Khan's wife was Bengali. That, Rehman Uncle said, would make the house appear safer to outsiders.

We were all packed into two rooms. The children weren't allowed out.

If the women went to the kitchen to make milk or fetch food, they spoke as little as possible and only in Bengali.

For two days, Rehman Uncle and his sons took turns checking on us.

But then, bad news came. Someone's informing on you, Rehman Uncle whispered. We must move you again soon.

Abbi nodded gravely. We've felt it too. We've felt it too. We've felt it too.

Find a way to India. Or Pakistan. Anywhere safe.

The race for survival had begun again.

That evening, Rehman Uncle returned, his face tight with concern.

I've heard a few groups are being sent back to India, he told Abbi softly. I'm gathering details. I'll try to get all of you out.

The hours crawled by.

At midnight, Rehman Uncle returned once again.

This time, his news was urgent.

Listen carefully, he told Abbi, lowering his voice.

We must leave tonight. At 2 A.M. Before the servants arrive. Someone has tipped off the Mukti Bahini about this place.

Abbi's face paled. But where can we go?

My son has spoken with the Mukti Bahini commander, Rehman Uncle continued.

They've ordered a raid here tomorrow, by 9 A.M.

My son has convinced them to delay it, but it won't be safe after dawn. We must move you before then.

Abbi closed his eyes briefly, taking a breath.

God will guide us, he whispered.

And so, once again, in the shadows of the night, the family prepared to run for their lives.

That night, no one slept.

We gathered our meager belongings in tense silence, eyes fixed on the door, waiting for Rehman Uncle. At exactly 2 A.M., he arrived.

An Indian Army truck followed behind him, his son seated beside him in their jeep.

Hurry, Rehman Uncle urged. We must leave before the world wakes up.

One by one, we climbed into the truck.

Under the watchful eyes of Rehman Uncle, his son, and the Indian soldiers, our convoy slipped into the darkness. It was unthinkable surreal.

The father of a Mukti Bahini commander, risking his own life to save the very people his comrades were hunting. But this was humanity. Not politics.

As the truck rolled through the abandoned streets, we were swallowed by an eerie silence.

All around us, Darkness. Stillness. Ruins.

Charred homes stood like skeletons against the black sky.

Burnt-out cars lay twisted along the roadsides.

Sometimes, worse. Bodies, Half-burned. Some are still hanging from trees. Women. Children. The elderly.

It was a landscape of nightmares.

The aftermath of rage, hatred, and betrayal.

We sat, frozen in fear, clutching each other.

The truck rumbled on, carrying us toward an unknown destination.

No one knew where we were going.

No one dared to hope.

Will this nightmare ever end? I wondered.

But no answer came.

Only the sound of tires over broken roads, and the silent prayers whispered into the night.

****

FROM DHAKA TO MEERUT

Our truck rumbled through the sleeping streets and finally entered the boundaries of the army cantonment. It was nearly five in the morning.

The convoy came to a halt.

Before us stood what had once been a Pakistani Army camp bustling with soldiers, now a sanctuary for people like us. People whom fate and the mercy of God had spared.

After the fall of Dhaka, two refugee camps had emerged in what was now Bangladesh.

One was this military camp, a fragile haven within the city.

The other lay far beyond the outskirts a place where desperation clung to every corner.

We were among the fortunate ones. By some grace, we had been brought here.

Here, freedom awaited us. Those who found themselves in the other camp were not so lucky.

That place had ceased to be a camp it had become a slum, a settlement of the forgotten. Poverty forced its people into crimes they once could never imagine.

Some camps, even worse, had simply vanished, their people swallowed by the chaos of war. We had survived. But the journey was not yet over. Freedom had a long road ahead.

The army camp where we now stood had once echoed with the voices of Pakistani soldiers but they had long since departed.

Only a handful remained, mostly the kitchen staff, men from Peshawar, clinging to the last threads of their duty.

This camp had become a holding ground for those who would soon be sent to India.

Though we didn't know it then, an agreement had been struck between the governments of Pakistan and India.

Pakistani prisoners held in India would be released in exchange for us.

But such diplomatic whispers never reached people like us.

We were focused only on survival.

This place was now our new shelter, though no one could say for how long.

How many more days of bread and breath had fate written for us?

The greatest worry for Abbi was clear. We had a roof over our heads. But no food and no way to cook it, even if we had some.

My parents stood silently outside the small room assigned to us, both lost in thought, the weight of our uncertain future pressing down on their shoulders.

Semi Apa and I whispered to each other, while Nadeem, Nazia, and Rehan played near Nani.

Suddenly, two men approached.

They wore the simple uniforms of army kitchen staff.

One was named Saad Mohammad, the other Khyal Mohammad. Khyal Mohammad lifted Nadeem into his arms and smiled.

Is this your child? he asked gently.

Yes, Abbi replied.

Khyal Mohammad's eyes softened.

I have a son the same age back home. He stays with his mother in Peshawar. Seeing your boy reminded me of him.

Turning to Ammi, he added, Sister, if you don't mind, may I ask you something?

Abbi nodded. Of course.

Where are you from? Sister, you look like someone from Peshawar.

Ammi smiled softly and said, my ancestors were Yousafzai Pathans. I came from the city of Bihar in India. My forefathers belonged to that region.

Then, lowering her voice, she added, Brother, we don't even have utensils to cook with. Only some banana leaves. Can you help us?

Saad Mohammad stepped forward, his eyes kind.

Sister, don't worry at all. Whatever you need, we will provide. We are Yousafzai Pathans too. You are our own people.

You truly remind me of my sister back home. As long as we are here, you were not worried about anything. Utensils, food, leave it all to us.

His words were not just a promise. They were a lifeline.

In that moment, strangers became family bound not by blood, but by shared roots and the unspoken understanding of those who had endured too much.

For the first time, my parents felt a flicker of relief in all this chaos and despair, at least someone was calling them their own and was ready to help.

Saad Mohammad Uncle and Khayal Mohammad Uncle brought cooking utensils for my mother. They also brought some food they had prepared for themselves tandoori roti and dal.

But not everyone in the camp shared their warmth. Some other families grumbled, why do they always get so much attention? Why are these people treated specially everywhere they go?

But as Ammi later told me, God gives honour to whom He wills. These people do not understand that.

The soldiers were not being generous out of pity.

They had seen in our family something that reminded them of their own homes their wives and children waiting far away.

Our family had three adults and five children. And by coincidence, we too were Yousafzai Pathans. But more than anything, they saw their children in us.

Once again, Khayal Mohammad Uncle and Saad Mohammad Uncle approached Ammi.

Sister, from today, you are our sister. As long as we are here, all your worries are ours.

Then they turned to Abbi and said, Brother, don't worry about food or supplies. We have plenty of grain and rations stored in tins. Whatever you need, just ask.

Nani raised her hands in prayer and blessed them from the depths of her heart. But once they left, she turned to Ammi and said sternly,

I am still very upset with your aunt, the mother-in-law who came with us.

Let it go, Amma, Ammi said gently. It was only a can of powdered milk. Look how God is helping us at every turn.

But my Nani shook her head. Her voice lowered into a whisper.

No, my child. It wasn't just a milk tin. Inside it, I had hidden more than half of my and your gold jewellery saved for times like these. That woman's carelessness cost us everything.

Ammi gasped, Amma! Why didn't you tell me before?

It was my mistake, Nani sighed. I didn't want to worry you. But listen carefully the rest of the jewellery is stitched inside the two pillows. Take care of them. And I have about 200 rupees left. Keep them safe for the children. If you can find any milk or supplies, buy them.

That evening, Rehman Uncle visited the camp. His face was serious.

My suspicions were right, he told Abbi. One of the servants did betray us. Just an hour after you all left Tamanna Sahib's house, Mukti Bahini raided it.

They didn't even inform my son, he continued. Because whoever leaked the information didn't trust him either.

Rehman Uncle stayed with us for a while, making sure we were safe and asking if we needed anything. Then, quietly, he took his leave.

We children were not yet used to this new world this military camp that smelled of dust, iron, and fear. There were no children our age in our group, no familiar friends.

The forty to forty-five people who had escaped with us were mostly adults. There was Maqbool Sahib's family from Lahore. Dr. Huda's family. Our Abbi's maternal uncle and aunt. Then there was Engineer Ejaz Sahib's family.

A few young boys no older than eighteen to twenty-four were with us too. Their families had either been killed or separated from them.

Aside from these, the camp held many other families. Strangers, really. People we didn't know, gathered here from across East Pakistan or what was now called Bangladesh. People from cities and towns we'd never heard of, all seeking refuge, all with their own stories of survival.

Some of them had children too, but since we were strangers to them, our parents didn't let us mingle.

We clung to one another, my siblings and I, drawing comfort from the only world we still recognized each other.

Everyone in the camp was tangled in their own worries, each wondering what fate had in store for them.

But for us children at least while we were with Uncle Khayal Mohammad and Uncle Saad Mohammad life inside the camp felt safe, almost happy.

Semi Appa, ever the shy one, spent most of her time close to Ammi and Nani. But Nadeem and I, we were inseparable from our two uncles. Their fellow kitchen staff, missing their own children back home, played with us too.

They taught us new games, laughed at our mischiefs, and for those fleeting moments, the heavy shadows of war seemed to lift.

Sometimes, Nazia and Rehan would join us. They were still very young, so Ammi and Nani kept them close. Semi Appa often entertained them when they fussed.

Our uncles watch our playful antics and smile, as though through us, they could remember their own children waiting for them in distant homes.

Yet, beneath this fragile happiness, the adults were weighed down with fears. Ammi and Nani's biggest worry was the little ones. Nazia and Rehan had no milk.

Nani would soak biscuits in tea or feed them rice water to keep their tiny bellies full.

Two days passed in the camp. Days that felt both long and short.

Then one morning, Rehman Uncle came again to visit. He asked about us his face full of concern and care.

Abbi told him, so far, things are not too difficult. The Indian Army's protection keeps us safe, but there's no certainty. We don't know how long we'll be allowed to stay here. My children are small, and food and clothing are becoming a worry. Please, help us find a way to be sent to India or Pakistan.

Rehman Uncle nodded thoughtfully. Alright, he said. I'll find out how long you'll have to stay here and when you might be sent to India or Pakistan. If not today, then tomorrow, I'll go with you to speak to the Indian Army and get the details.

The next day, true to his word, Rehman Uncle took Abbi to the Indian Army camp. There, they met with an officer. The officer listened patiently, then reassured them,
We will be moving you out of Dhaka soon. As soon as we have information about when and where everyone will be sent, we will notify you.

There was relief in the officer's words, but uncertainty still loomed over us like a dark cloud.

Abbi and Rehman Uncle returned to the camp. Another day passed. Then another. We waited. No news came.

Then, quite suddenly, one day, two officers arrived at the camp. They went around asking people for Abbi. Word spread quickly through the rows of tents and shelters, until finally, they reached our barracks.

Abbi grew a little uneasy. A quiet fear crept into his voice as he stepped forward and asked,

Why are you looking for me?

One of the officers smiled kindly.
Actually, he said, I'm from the same place in India as you. Perhaps you don't recognize me now. I'm Lakhan Singh's eldest son the one who joined the army.

For a moment, Abbi looked puzzled. And then memory came rushing back like a warm breeze on a cold day.

Lakhan Singh.

Of course. He had been a family friend once, a man who had taught Hindi to Abbi when he was just a boy. Lakhan Singh had close relation with my grandfather back when he had been posted as a doctor in the town of Neura, Bihar. The past had come calling at the door of a war refugee camp.

Lakhan Singh's son smiled gently and began to explain, When I returned from meeting my father, he gave me this letter. He told me, if you find my friend's son in Dhaka, give him this letter and let me know how he and his family are doing.

I could not ignore my father's words. So, for the past month, I have been searching for you. By God's grace, I have finally found you.

Then he looked at Abbi, his eyes kind and sincere. Tell me now. How can I help you?

Abbi's voice quivered slightly, if it's possible, could you take us with you to India?

The officer nodded thoughtfully. I'm returning to India tomorrow. I will do everything I can to take you along. But I'll need to get approval from my superiors.

If I don't return tomorrow, you will know that I failed. But I promise, at the very least, I will deliver news of your safety to your father.

Please write him a letter. That way, I can pass along your words in your own handwriting."

Without wasting a moment, Abbi quickly scribbled a letter. His hands trembled slightly not from fear, but from the weight of hope.

He handed it over. I'll pray for your success. May God open the way for us.

Lakhan Singh's son took the letter carefully, as if it were something precious.

I'll be going now, he said softly. Pray that I succeed in taking you with me and that I can finally ease your father's worries. He has been deeply concerned.

And with that, he left. That day, we all witnessed a rare and beautiful thing the enduring bond between a Hindu and a Muslim, a friendship so deep that even war could not shatter it.

After Lakhan Singh's son left, the entire day and night passed in restless waiting.

Abbi, Ammi and Nani sat in anxious hope, eyes turning toward the gate every time a footstep echoed nearby. But no news came. He did not return.

It became painfully clear that even his hands were tied that despite his best intentions, there was nothing more he could do.

The fragile thread of hope they had held onto began to fray, yet none of them let despair take over.

Just as the shadows of disappointment grew heavier, Rehman Uncle returned to the camp.

Abbi immediately spoke to him, explaining what had happened. Rehman Uncle's son listened carefully and then gave a suggestion.

All the people in this camp should write a petition sign it and request the Indian Army headquarters for help in getting out of here.

Abbi wasted no time. He quickly drafted a letter. Soon, every person in the camp added their signature to the desperate plea.

The letter was handed to the Indian Army personnel stationed at the camp, who promised to forward it to headquarters. Days passed with heavy hearts and silent prayers.

At last, a response arrived. The message was brief but life-changing.

The trapped people in East Pakistan would be moved. Your camp is included.

Abbi anxiously asked, where will we be taken?

The reply came: To Pakistan.

At that moment, for the first time in weeks, a faint light flickered in the darkness.

Fifteen days had quietly slipped by in the Pakistan Army camp. Then, one morning, the long-awaited announcement came. All families, be ready. Within a week, the evacuation will begin.

The camp buzzed with cautious hope.

There were almost five thousand souls sheltering within the camp's boundaries. Soon, names were being called. Group by group, families were ushered toward the next phase of their uncertain journey.

Our family's name appeared in the third list. Four more days passed in tense anticipation.

Finally, our turn arrived. A large military truck pulled up, its engine rumbling like the drumbeat of fate. Ten families about fifty people in total were told to gather their belongings and prepare to leave.

Ammi, Abbi and Nani hurriedly gathered our possessions, tying up loose items with cloth and rope.

In her youthful innocence and quick thinking, Semi Appa bundled together all the potatoes and tomatoes into a bedsheet, slinging it over her shoulder like a young warrior carrying supplies into battle.

We children grabbed whatever food and small items we could clutch in our little hands.

Soon, we were all aboard the truck.

As it roared to life and began rolling forward, the city's haunted streets unfolded before us roads heavy with fear, silence, hatred, and the lingering scent of violence.

The Maukti Bahini fighters spotted our convoy and surged toward us, shouting threats, ready to strike.

But on either side of our truck, Indian Army jeeps flanked us, providing cover and protection.

I noticed the glares of hatred burning in the eyes of those onlookers. And in our eyes-only questions. What was our crime?

Was it merely a difference in language that made them want to kill us?

Was this the Pakistan that had been promised in the name of Islam?

The truck rumbled slowly forward, each rotation of the wheels mirroring the pounding of our anxious hearts.

No one spoke. No one dared ask what awaited us next. Suddenly, the truck halted near Dhaka Railway Station.

We peered out cautiously. The entire station was surrounded encircled by Indian Army soldiers standing in formation, rifles poised.

But outside the protective ring, a growing crowd had gathered. The faces were angry. Among them, unmistakably, were Mukti Bahini fighters.

The Indian Army began moving us forward, shielding us from every side as we approached the waiting train.

The air filled with jeers and insults.

Āmāra sōnāra dēśa. Tumi ēkhāna thēkē calē yā'ō.

(Get out from our golden land)

Suddenly, stones began to fly.

A few thudded against the truck, then more smashed against the train's metal sides. We huddled closer together, shielding the little ones instinctively.

The soldiers didn't flinch. They kept urging us along briskly, surrounding us like a human barricade.

We were guided toward a sealed train. No one will open the windows; the soldiers barked in both Bengali and Urdu as they hurried us aboard.

Our family was ushered into a single carriage with about sixty others crowded, breathless, clinging to what little hope we still had.

In the neighbouring compartments, more families from other parts of the city were being packed in.

Once everyone was aboard, Indian Army personnel climbed into each carriage, standing guard. Their faces were stern but not unkind. The doors slammed shut.

For a moment, it was silent except for the muted cries of children and the quiet sobbing of mothers holding their little ones tightly. The train was ready to depart. But none of us knew exactly where it was taking us or what new trials lay ahead.

Once everyone was seated, the train slowly began to move, its wheels grinding forward as if dragging us toward an uncertain destiny.

Father leaned toward one of the Indian army officers and asked cautiously,
Where are we being taken?

The soldier replied gently,

You're being transported to Narayanganj.

The train windows remained tightly shut. Not a breath of fresh air stirred inside. Every so often, the sharp thud of bricks crashing against the windows echoed through the carriage. The air was thick, not only with heat and the suffocating closeness of too many people, but with fear. No one dared open the windows wherever the train passed, angry locals hurled stones at us.

Āmāra sōnāra dēśa Bangladesh! (Our golden land, Bangladesh!)
They shouted, cursing us, threatening us with death for a crime we had never committed.

In those desperate moments, the Indian army soldiers truly appeared to us like guardian angels, pulling us from the very jaws of death.

Finally, after what felt like an eternity, the train arrived at Narayanganj. But what awaited us there was even more terrifying.

We had to disembark and walk a short distance to reach the waiting riverboat. Yet the path from the train to the boat felt like crossing the razor-thin Bridge of Doom itself.

On either side of the line, government workers gathered the very same people who, before the fall of Dhaka, had abandoned their posts at the call of Sheikh Mujib's strike and had been replaced by non-Bengalis.

Now, after the fall of Dhaka, they were seeking revenge, identifying and dragging out any non-Bengalis they recognized to beat or kill them on the spot. With every step, life and death walked beside us.

The Indian soldiers surrounded us, trying to shield us, but despite their efforts, people from the mob managed to grab hold of someone now and then. Death lurked everywhere, yet the soldiers pressed us forward.

Among the mob, Abbi suddenly spotted a familiar face Shamsuddin, a PIA staff member who had once worked closely with him. Shamsuddin had also gone on strike and lost his job before the war. He knew Abbi and Ammi very well.

Abbi's face drained of colour.

Quickly, he threw a cloth over his head, balanced a heavy trunk upon it, and disguised himself as a porter. He whispered to Ammi and Nani to cover their faces with their sari pallus.

Carrying the trunk as if it were a daily burden, Abbi led the way. Ammi, Nani, and we children followed silently, our lips moving in constant prayer.

Suddenly, Shamsuddin stepped directly into Abbi's path.

For one heart-stopping moment, Abbi thought everything was lost. But fate had another plan. One of Shamsuddin's companions spotted someone else and pulled him from the line. They barely glanced at Abbi and moved on.

We didn't look back. We kept moving forward, knowing only that survival lay ahead, not behind.

Even we children had learned wisdom beyond our years. Holding hands, praying under our breath, we reached the riverboat.

But even boarding the boat was a battle. Mukti Bahini fighters tried to snatch people from the crowd, pulling and pushing amidst the chaos.

In that mad scramble, with the little strength they had left, Abbi, Ammi and Nani lifted us the children and our precious few belongings onto the boat. Around us, everywhere, was confusion and terror.

Even in the river, Mukti Bahini patrols floated in small boats, ready to seize anyone they could. Life was still dangling by the thinnest of threads.

By the grace of God, we finally made it onto the riverboat. As our feet touched the deck, a deep breath of relief escaped us all. But there was barely space to stand, let alone sit. Every inch of the boat was already crowded with people. More families continued to climb aboard, and no one had been assigned a specific place.

The boat carried all kinds of people. Some were small business owners, but many were doctors, engineers, and highly educated professionals the very people the Mukti Bahini were hunting down and killing.

They raided everywhere, searching especially for these educated men and women. Even now, they attempted to storm the boat.

Our group of sixty included such individuals, making us a prime target. The Indian Army provided us with special protection because of this clear danger.

Among us was a gentleman with a 19-year-old daughter. As the boat filled, the girl suddenly decided to disembark to buy something, telling no one. At that very moment, another young woman stepped off the boat just ahead of her.

The Mukti Bahini fighters were waiting. In the blink of an eye, they seized one girl. The Indian soldiers rushed to rescue her, but by the time they reached the spot, it was too late.

The grief that swept over the boat was overwhelming. We all knew what fate awaited those poor girls. In that moment, any remaining illusion that we were safe was shattered.

We realized we were still trapped between life and death even now, on the threshold of what we had hoped was freedom.

Abbi rushed forward and grabbed the other 19-year-old girl just in time, pulling her back onto the boat. Instead of gratitude, she lashed out at him with angry words, her fear turning into defiance.

Without hesitation, Abbi slapped her across the face.

Go, he said sharply, his voice trembling with a mix of anger and terror, go if you wish to die! Were you blind? Did you not see what just happened to the other girl before your very eyes?

Turning to the girl's father, he added sternly, keep your daughter close. Because of her recklessness, all sixty of us, under the Army's protection, could be killed. Right now, everyone on this boat wants only to survive. If even one person, tempted by a handful of food, betrays us to the Mukti Bahini, we will all die. Tie her to your side if you must.

A heavy silence followed his words. In that desperate time, no one could afford foolishness. Survival was not just a hope anymore it was a discipline.

The army officers, too, scolded the girl and her father. You people, especially this group of sixty from the kitchen staff and government services, are very important to us, one of them said sharply.

Be careful and do not bring trouble upon us all. Stay aboard the ship. Speak to no one outside your group, and stay away from the balcony railings. (We would later learn that most of us were semi-government and government employees).

That was why the Army had assigned special protection to our group. Among us were also staff from the military canteen.

Soon after, the officers arranged for our group to move to the upper deck of the ship. Our family was given a cabin a special gesture, they said, because Mr. Rehman had vouched for us and requested special care.

Besides, the officer in charge seemed to have developed a soft spot for us children. Perhaps we reminded him of his own family far away, whom he hadn't seen in months.

When the chaos of the move settled, we peered out from the upper deck at the open sea. What we saw sent a chill down our spines. The water was dotted with swollen, round shapes drifting with the tide.

Abbi, concerned, asked one of the army men, what is floating in the water?

The soldier sighed heavily. Bodies, he said quietly. The sea is carrying the dead now.

He paused, then added, there are more people coming aboard over the next two days. The ship will remain at the dock a little longer. You must be extremely cautious. Danger still lurks everywhere.

Those two days felt endless. Every few hours, Mukti Bahini leaders would board the ship to conduct searches, and the Indian Army could not always stop them.

They were hunting for government and semi-government employees, pulling them from their families and taking them away often never to be seen again.

Seeing the danger closing in, Abbi made a difficult decision. He gathered all official documents, the papers proving his PIA employment, our family identification, everything and tore them into pieces, casting them into the sea.

Ammi gasped in alarm. You've destroyed all our proofs! How will we manage without those papers? What will we do when we reach the next place?

Abbi's eyes were heavy with the weight of his choice. No piece of paper is worth risking your life, my life, the children, or Amma's, he said quietly. I would rather face the world empty-handed than let a single document become the reason we're dragged away.

As he spoke, the footsteps of the Mukti Bahini echoed closer. Suddenly, they were upon us, storming the upper deck. They began rummaging through our belongings, questioning Abbi harshly.

What do you do? Where are your papers? Show us proof of your work! they demanded.

Abbi stood calmly. I have no papers. I am just a poor man traveling with his family.

The men searched thoroughly but found nothing. After a tense few minutes, they left, leaving behind the cold weight of fear.

For now, we were safe but everyone knew the danger had only been delayed, not erased.

On the ship, we were at least receiving three meals a day, a small mercy in the middle of so much fear and uncertainty. Yet the food was barely enough to keep hunger at bay.

In the morning, we were each given a tiny cup of tea and a small puri. It was hardly a meal for an adult, let alone for growing children. Still, it was enough to keep us alive.

The younger ones Nazia, Rehan, and even Nadeem, would often clutch their stomachs and cry softly from hunger. My parents, with heavy hearts yet determined, always gave up half food of their own portions to the children's.

Noon and evening meals brought a small helping of lentils and bread, just enough to give the body the illusion of nourishment.

No one complained. Hunger became just another quiet companion, like fear and hope, constant presences that followed us everywhere.

Abbi told Nani and Ammi, take down the sack of potatoes that Semi tied up. But both Nani and Ammi refused. We don't know what lies ahead, they said firmly.

We'll keep the potatoes with us. Something must have been running through their minds, some foresight or fear that they didn't voice aloud.

We children were not allowed near the ship's railings. So, Nadeem and I began rummaging through our belongings to find something to play with. Soon enough, we found the golf balls that Semi Appa had secretly tucked away among the luggage.

Nadeem and I sat facing each other, rolling the ball back and forth between us. Semi Appa joined in too. Nazia and Rehan were asleep, curled up near Nani.

Suddenly, the ship gave a slight lurch. The ball slipped from our hands and rolled away. We chased after it, and then I saw the sight that has never left me, not even after all these years. And perhaps that was why the soldiers and the elders always forbade us from going near the railings.

Far out across the water, boats drifted silently and everywhere, bloated bodies floated alongside them. Bodies of Children, Women and Men all had fallen victim to the river's dark embrace. Their corpses had swollen and decayed in the water, a terrible testament to the slaughter that had swept our homeland.

On those small boats sat Mukti Bahini fighters. They circled the ship like silent shadows, their eyes watchful, waiting. As Nadeem and I caught sight of the horror below, an involuntary scream escaped our lips.

Hearing us, Abbi and some army guards rushed toward us, their faces taut with fear. Abbi scolded us sharply. How many times have I told you not to come near the railings!

But then he followed the direction of our trembling fingers. The colour drained from his face. At once, he pulled us back roughly and shielded us from the view.

The soldiers stationed on the floor below surged forward. Some ran toward the upper deck, rifles ready. The ship's horn blared a long, deep wail of alarm. Panic rippled through the passengers.

What Nadeem and I had seen was not just the floating corpses or the circling boats. No. It was death itself, creeping closer.

The Mukti Bahini had thrown grappling ropes onto the side of our ship and were climbing aboard. They wore only lungis around their waists, swords strapped to their backs, curved daggers glinting at their hips. Their dark, lean bodies swayed as they scaled the ropes like predators closing in on helpless prey.

If that golf ball had not fallen into the water If we had not screamed.
They would have reached the deck unnoticed. And no one would have survived.

Our cries alerted the soldiers, who opened fire immediately, dropping the attackers into the sea before they could board. Even as they fell, the Mukti Bahini cursed the soldiers and spat defiance. Once again, our faith in God grew even stronger.

Abbi gathered us close. His voice trembled. I scolded these children so much for stealing that golf ball, he whispered. But now I understand. God used that little ball to save not just us but countless lives aboard this ship. Just like He once used a wristwatch and a box of cigarettes to save me in Dhaka.

By the grace of God, two long days somehow passed.

The Mukti Bahini fighters kept returning, boarding the ship again and again, inspecting every corner. They seemed determined to find any remaining government officials hiding among us. Only when they were fully satisfied that none remained did they finally give permission for the vessel to move forward.

At last, the ship stirred, pulling away from the cursed shores. But those two days, only we knew how we had survived them.
The children, innocent, unaware managed to sleep. But the adults could not close their eyes.

Each hour felt like a battle against fear itself. Someone was always awake, taking shifts alongside the Indian Army soldiers to stand guard.

By now, none of us saw ourselves as mere Pakistanis or the soldiers as merely Indian. There was only *one* thing that bound us together now is humanity. And it was in the name of that humanity that they risked their lives to protect us. They had their loved ones waiting for them too.

Even the food we received was strictly monitored. The ship's original crew had been dismissed. Instead, the men from the Pakistani Army kitchen, our old companions were now preparing our meals. There were fears that someone among the ship's staff might betray us, poisoning the food.

Safety was a fragile thing. Trust even more so.

The ship had set course for Khulna, but none of us knew exactly where we were being taken or where it would eventually stop.

When we finally docked at the Khulna port, the ship came to a halt beside a vast grain warehouse. This empty, echoing structure was to become our next refuge.

We disembarked under the constant watch of the Indian Army soldiers, who never left our side. They herded us carefully into the warehouse, urging everyone inside quickly and firmly. As we entered, people simply settled wherever they could find space.

The warehouse doors remained open, though the soldiers kept telling everyone to stay away from them.

Among us were many children who had been separated from their parents, or whose parents had been left behind. Despite repeated warnings, a few of the older boys kept gravitating toward the entrance, hoping perhaps to spot a loved one or to find an escape.

Then, right before our eyes, the Mukti Bahini fighters lunged from the shadows and dragged two boys away, stabbing them mercilessly with knives.

A scream went up. The soldiers rushed forward and slammed the warehouse doors shut. Inside, the silence was heavy with fear. We had almost no food. All we had were the potatoes my sister Samina had wrapped up before our journey, our only sustenance.

Those who had brought other food guarded it closely. In this desperate time, everyone had to fend for themselves. No one knew how long we would remain in this place, or if we would ever leave.

That evening, as hunger gnawed at us, we children began to cry especially Nadeem, Nazia, and little Rehan. Abbi grew anxious.
I'll try to find something to eat, he said to Ammi, but who will give it to us? Who should I even ask?

Ammi replied softly, we still have some potatoes, but no pot or stove to cook them. Can you find someone who might lend us a stove?

I'll see what I can do, Abbi sighed, lighting what was now his last cigarette. He smoked slowly, eyes scanning the crowd around us.

Seeing us children crying, Uncle Khayal Muhammad came over. What's wrong, sister? Is there nothing to eat?

Ammi nodded helplessly. We have potatoes but no pot or stove. How can I boil them for the children?

Khayal Muhammad Uncle shook his head sympathetically. I have a stove and a pot but no food. You take them and cook the potatoes for the little ones.

He brought over the stove and a pot, with just enough oil left to last two days if used carefully. Ammi quickly boiled six potatoes. She gave the children theirs and split one large potato into three pieces for Abbi, herself and Nani.

When Uncle Khayal Muhammad and his companions were offered food, they refused and said.

We adults can manage, but these children cannot endure hunger. Who knows how long we'll be here?

The Indian soldiers had at least arranged water for us. No one was allowed outside. The suffocating air inside the sealed warehouse pressed down on us. The children grew restless, crying out from hunger. As time stretched on, despair crept into every heart.

What will happen now? Where are they taking us?
Are these soldiers our friends or will they betray us?

No one knew what was happening beyond the walls. Armed guards surrounded the warehouse, their presence a constant reminder of the danger outside.

Occasionally, distant gunfire and shouts broke the tense silence. The soldiers told us little except that the Mukti Bahini and angry mobs kept trying to attack, but the guards were holding them back. They said they were waiting for new orders.

Days or perhaps just two or three blurred together. We lost count.

Then, one night, sometime deep into the early hours, soldiers entered the warehouse.

Stay quiet! they commanded. No shouting. No crying. Hold on to your families. Keep the little ones from making any noise. No torches, no lights. Follow us silently.

As always, I, Semi Appa, and Nadeem were strictly told not to utter a sound. Little Nazia and Rehan had their mouths gently covered to keep them from crying.

When we stepped outside, the darkness was absolute, save for the bright moon overhead as though God Himself had placed it there to light our path. Under the moon's glow, we formed a line and began walking.

We didn't know how long we walked fifteen, twenty minutes perhaps. The adults carried the smallest children when they grew too weary.

Finally, the soldiers halted us. More guards closed in around us, ahead, behind, and on both sides. We had reached what appeared to be the outer area of a railway station. Several trains stood silently on side tracks.

We were ordered to board. It wasn't easy. In the darkness, women and children struggled, but eventually, everyone managed to climb aboard the sealed train.

Inside, there were no working lights or fans. Abbi searched the luggage for a candle, but a soldier stopped him.

Not yet, he whispered.

Abbi gathered Ammi, Nani and the children by sound and touch in the dark. He called each name softly, making sure no one was missing.

Our original group of sixty remained together in one carriage, while others boarded elsewhere. Throughout this journey, we'd noticed something our group was always given better care and separate accommodations. Perhaps it was because of the doctors, engineers, and civil servants among us or maybe because of Rehman Uncle. Or perhaps it was just the will of God.

Six Indian Army soldiers accompanied us in the carriage. Only one door remained open, and none of the carriages were linked. The shutters were closed from the inside.

The air was heavy and stifling. The sealed windows and darkness only deepened the suffocation.

One of the soldiers turned to Abbi. You can light the candle now, so the children won't be frightened. Once the train moves, fresh air will come through. But no one must try to open a window until then.

My little brother Rehan and Nazia, still just infants, squirmed restlessly in Ammi's and Nani's laps. The stifling heat and lack of food were unbearable, especially for the little ones who still needed milk.

Finally, by the mercy of God the train began to move, slowly at first, carrying us toward yet another unknown destination.

No one knew how long the train had been moving when it finally slowed and came to a stop. The windows were still sealed, so we had no idea where we were.

When Abbi quietly inquired, word came back, we've reached Khulna Railway Station. The engine is being changed.

We waited in tense silence until the soldiers confirmed that a new engine had been attached. Only much later would we learn that this was actually an Indian train engine coupled to our train.

It was around three or four in the morning when the train once again rumbled forward into the darkness, headed to a destination none of us knew.

Every mind harboured the same silent, fearful question, when will this journey end? Where are they taking us now?

Abbi cautiously asked one of the soldiers, do you know where we're going?

The soldier shook his head.

We honestly don't know exactly where the train is headed. But from what we've been told, eventually you will all be taken to Pakistan.

An hour later, another announcement came, First, you'll be transported to India. From there, you will be sent to Pakistan. Some people felt a wave of relief. Others grew anxious, weighed down by uncertainty. But all were united in offering silent gratitude to God. Whatever lay ahead, it surely couldn't be worse than the nightmare we were leaving behind.

The train surged forward steadily through the night. The suffocating heat inside the carriage began to ease.

As dawn broke, the women and children stirred from uneasy sleep. The men remained awake, their minds heavy with unknown fears.

Little Nadeem and Rehan climbed down from the berth and began playing near the soldiers. One soldier was seated by the sealed window.

Uncle, Nadeem chirped, can you open the window? We want to see outside. And we're hungry!

One of the soldiers smiled gently. We'll open it soon, little one.

About half an hour passed before the soldiers tried to open the window. Despite their efforts, it wouldn't budge. Finally, one soldier gave the frame a strong kick with his boot. Part of the window cracked open.

To our surprise, we children clapped joyfully at the noise.

Uncle, Nadeem exclaimed, eyes shining, your shoe is so powerful, when I grow up, I'll get a pair just like it

The soldiers chuckled at his innocence. To keep the children entertained, they forced open two or three more windows the same way.

Fresh air rushed in at last, and for the first time in days, we felt a small taste of freedom.

The train continued its relentless journey for quite some time before the news spread through the carriages we had crossed into India.

At that moment, a wave of relief washed over us. We felt, for the first time, that we were in safe hands. The suffocating fear began to melt away.

Ammi, Abbi and Nani began reminiscing about their childhoods, their parents, and the homes they had left behind.

For some reason, it suddenly felt like, in just a few hours, everyone would be reunited with their past lives and their long-lost homes.

But this was only a dream. Reality had more trials in store.

After what felt like an endless journey, our train finally halted at the outer signal of Sealdah station.

An Indian Army officer approached Abbi and the other men. Have you eaten? Do you have any food?

Abbi shook his head. We have nothing.

Wait here. No one is to leave the train, the officer instructed firmly.

One of the soldiers left and soon returned with food supplies a few basic items, including some crispy salted snacks known as *namak pare*. He handed them to Ammi. Feed these to the little ones.

Nazia and Rehan, just toddlers at a year and a half and two and a half years old, nibbled on the softened namak pare, which Nani had dipped in water to make easier for them to eat. Milk was still impossible to find.

Once everyone had eaten, Abbi looked out of the window. Large hoses were spraying water across the train's surface they seemed to be cleaning it.

A few people from our carriage requested permission to bathe under the rushing water.

After considering for a moment, the soldiers granted permission to Abbi, Nadeem, and a couple of others, but made sure they were carefully watched from all sides.

Abbi, Nadeem, and Rehan enjoyed their wash, laughing for the first time in what felt like forever

But soon, the soldiers noticed some people approaching from a distance.

The soldiers quickly ordered everyone back onto the train. This isn't the time to be outside.

When the train reaches Sealdah station, no one is to speak to any vendors or buy anything, they warned. Safety still hung by a thread.

After a short while, the train began moving again and rolled into Sealdah Station.

As soon as it stopped, the soldiers began counting everyone in each compartment to ensure that no one had disembarked and that no unknown passengers had climbed aboard.

But as the train halted, the station vendors (pheri walas) rushed toward us, just as they did when any train arrived. A crowd gathered quickly.

When the army soldiers refused to let anyone approach or board the train, some vendors began calling out, where are you coming from? Where are you going?

Someone from one of the compartments replied, we've come from Bangladesh. We are going to Pakistan.

That one sentence was enough to spark chaos. Suddenly, angry slogans erupted from the crowd. Shouts of protest and hatred rang out against us.

The soldiers quickly pushed forward, dispersing the vendors and forcing the crowd back.

They warned everyone inside, no one is to buy anything from the hawkers. Your lives are in danger. Food could easily be poisoned.

The children, however, couldn't understand the danger. Seeing all the food being sold on the platform, they began crying out in hunger.

One soldier approached our compartment, his voice kind but firm.
We are not your enemies. But we fear that some disguised as hawkers might try to harm you. They could poison the food. That's why we are stopping you.

But don't worry, he added. We will go outside ourselves, inspect the food, and bring it to you.

The soldiers left the compartment. After some time, they returned with a few packets of sealed food.

Before handing it to us, they broke open a package and placed it in front of a stray dog wandering the platform.

Only when the dog ate the food without harm did they distribute it to the passengers.

Finally, a sense of relief swept over us. The children stopped crying, their small stomachs temporarily satisfied. For now, we were safe. But the shadows of fear still lingered.

The train remained at Sealdah *Station* for nearly two hours.

It must have been around one or two in the afternoon when the train finally pulled away from Sealdah.

I no longer remember whether our journey from Sealdah lasted one day, two days, or four, or whether the train meandered from place to place before finally arriving at *Gaya*.

All I recall is that the journey from Sealdah to Gaya felt endless. At every stop, we faced similar troubles. The train would only move forward when the tracks were clear. Perhaps the railway authorities had received special instructions, though we didn't know what they were.

Thanks to the kindness of the army, we never lacked food or water during the journey. It was close to midnight, perhaps around twelve, when the train finally rolled into *Gaya*.

As the train crossed into Bihar, the hearts of all those aboard who hailed from the region began to race.

For a fleeting moment, Abbi considered leaping off the train with the whole family. The train was moving slowly as it passed through *Gaya*, and it seemed like an opportunity to escape.

But Ammi stopped him. Running away isn't easy not with the children, she whispered firmly.

The train crawled along, occasionally halting at outer signals before picking up speed again, only to brush past stations without stopping.

Somewhere beyond Gaya, I cannot recall the exact place, the train was passing by open fields at a snail's pace when, suddenly, the sharp crack of gunfire rang out. All the soldiers aboard sprang to alert at once.

The train came to an abrupt halt. One soldier from each compartment stepped down. We were strictly forbidden from approaching the doors.

For a tense while, we sat in fearful silence, straining to understand what was happening. Eventually, the soldiers returned and the train resumed its journey.

At last, after much anxious questioning, one of them explained:
Some boys from another carriage tried to jump off the train and flee. We warned them to stop, but they didn't listen. We had no choice. They could've been spies, we couldn't take that risk.

The train rolled steadily forward, leaving Bihar behind and eventually halting at Mughal Sarai.

At Mughal Sarai, our train was placed on a middle track, and as always, we were forbidden from buying anything or speaking to strangers.

We sat quietly, watching the station's activity. Abbi looked out longingly, wishing we too could roam freely on this land where he had spent his childhood.

Semi Appa noticed some vegetables at a stall and curiously asked what they were.

One of the soldiers overheard her and asked, is she hungry?
Samina nodded silently.

The soldier kindly bought some spiced potatoes and small *kachoris* for us. Before handing them over, as always, he first fed a little to a dog or cat to ensure it was safe and not poisoned.

The food tasted delicious so much so that to this day, Ammi and Semi Appa still recall that simple meal with fondness.

At Mughal Sarai, the passengers were once again allowed to bathe using water hoses at the station. Soon, the train chugged out of Mughal Sarai.

Abbi went to speak with one of the soldiers. Where exactly are we headed? We've been traveling for so many days now. The soldier gave no reply.

As the train rumbled along toward an unknown destination, the children had grown friendly with the Indian Army soldiers who accompanied us. They often sat in their laps, laughing and playing, or ran up and down the cramped train carriage. Time passed slowly, heavy with uncertainty.

Finally, the train, stopping at countless stations and signals, reached Aligarh. There, we learned for the first time that our destination was not Pakistan, as we had thought. We were being taken to *Meerut*. A wave of confusion swept over Abbi and the other men.

We were told we'd be sent to Pakistan, Abbi said, frowning deeply. Why are they taking us to Meerut?

But when they asked the soldiers, no answers came. The soldiers simply shook their heads. We've told you everything we know, they replied. What little information we had, we shared so you wouldn't be frightened. Now, we've been given no further details.

From Aligarh to Meerut, the journey stretched across what felt like days. Perhaps it was only a day or two, but it was hard to tell anymore. The train crept forward, often stopping for hours in deserted places. At every halt, the soldiers warned us not to leave the carriages.

Finally, the train pulled into the army cantonment station at Meerut just as dusk settled across the winter sky. The date had blurred in our minds had it been fifteen days since we left East Pakistan? Twenty? We could not say.

All we knew was that we had escaped the jaws of death. But whether we had arrived at safety or merely traded one uncertainty for another, we did not know.

Outside the train, heavily armed soldiers stood guard, surrounding the area. Our hearts sank. What awaited us now? We had been passengers fleeing for freedom. Now, it seemed we were captives once again.

****

PRISONER OF WAR - CAMP NO. 51

When the passengers saw the sheer number of soldiers at the Meerut cantonment station, their rifles gleaming in the fading light, fear spread like wildfire through the train. One by one, families began shutting the windows of their carriages, as if a closed window might shield them from whatever fate awaited outside.

We, too, felt that chill of dread. Yet, somehow by God's grace alone Abbi found the courage that others could not.

An announcement echoed again and again over the loudspeakers, urging everyone to disembark. But no one moved. A dark thought haunted every mind: What if they've brought us here just to kill us?

Ammi clutched at Abbi's arm, trying to hold him back. Please, don't go, she whispered, her voice trembling. Stay here. Don't open that door.

But Abbi gently pried her hand away. God is watching over us, he said calmly. Let me at least find out what's happening.

Taking a deep breath, he stepped to the door. As the others cowered inside, he slid it open and peered out into the unknown.

The loudspeaker blared again: All passengers, please disembark immediately. Yet still, no one moved.

Abbi stood at the door, gathering his courage. He pressed his palms together in a respectful "*Pranam*" toward the soldiers outside.

One of them gestured. Don't be afraid. Come here.

With hesitant steps, Abbi descended from the train and approached the officers standing nearby. The crisp winter air was tense with uncertainty.

One of the officers spoke up. What's your name?

Shamim Ahmed, Abbi answered, his voice steady despite the fear gripping his chest.

You've come from Bangladesh, and you'll be heading to Pakistan. But which part of India are you originally from?

Bihar, Abbi replied.

The officer nodded. What did you do back in East Pakistan?

I worked for Pakistan International Airlines. P.I.A.

The officer consulted a clipboard. His questions seemed casual, but Abbi noticed he was checking a list, a list that already had names written on it. It was clear they knew more than they let on, perhaps trying to ease the fear that hung over the refugees like a shadow.

Are there only civilians in your carriage? the officer asked.

Yes, sir. All civilians. At least in my carriage. I can't speak for the others, Abbi replied honestly.

The officer nodded again, then frowned slightly. Why aren't people getting off the train?

They're scared, sir, Abbi admitted. We've been through too much. People are afraid they'll be taken off and killed.

The officer's face softened slightly. He turned and handed Abbi a microphone. Take this, he said.

Tell everyone it's safe. Tell them to disembark. No one will be harmed.

Taking the microphone, Abbi called out clearly into the cold evening air.

Saad-ur-Rehman Khan, can you hear me?

A voice answered from the crowd. Yes, Bhai.

Abbi took a breath and raised his voice so all the carriages could hear.

Everyone, listen carefully. There's no danger here. Look at me, I am standing safely among them. These soldiers are here for our protection. They will help us move forward from here. There's no reason to be afraid. Please, everyone, disembark. We are safe now, and we must keep moving.

At first, there was a hush the silence of people weighing fear against hope. Then slowly, the passengers from our carriage began to step down onto the platform. Abbi returned and carefully helped Ammi, Nani, and us children down from the train.

One by one, the other carriages emptied too. Families huddled together, their faces wary but relieved.

Once everyone had gathered, an officer stepped forward. Those with families, please stand together. Young men and women traveling alone, please gather over there.

A ripple of panic stirred through the crowd again.

What now? Are they planning to separate us to harm us?

But the officer raised a calming hand.

There is no need to fear. You will all be transported by truck. Families will stay together. No one will be separated.

Still, the crowd was uneasy. Murmurs rose.

The young men and women traveling alone they must also stay with us. We cannot let them go alone.

The officer nodded. Yes. We will load the trucks so no one is divided from their group.

After much persuasion and reassurance, people finally agreed. Slowly, the process of boarding the trucks began. Each vehicle carried several families along with the single young men and women.

Soldiers stood watch; their weapons slung but their manner calm. It was clear they understood how fragile this hope was, how close to breaking the trust of these battered people might be.

Once everyone had boarded the trucks, the convoy rumbled into motion. We couldn't see much through the dark canvas covers, just shadows and the occasional flash of streetlights. From the driver, Abbi learned we were heading toward a military cantonment.

The night was deep, silent, and heavy with fear when the trucks finally rolled to a stop. Soldiers moved about, their boots crunching against gravel. We had arrived at a military camp which, we later learned, had been designated *Camp No. 51*.

One by one, families and individuals disembarked, clutching their belongings tightly, their faces pale and drawn in the dim light.

An officer's voice cut through the tense night air. Women and children to one side. Men to the other.

A ripple of fear passed through the crowd. People began to cry out in panic.

They've brought us here to kill us! We won't be separated! We'll stay together!

The murmurs swelled into a frightened chorus. Ammi gripped her children tighter. Some men stepped in front of their families, defiant.

But amidst the rising commotion, a senior officer arrived, observing the scene quietly before raising his hand for calm. No one will be harmed. You will not be separated tonight.

So, that night, each family was assigned a separate barrack. Fear lingered in the air, but for now, relief prevailed.

Later, food was distributed a simple meal of mixed vegetables and roti. But there were no plates or utensils. Soldiers gathered banana leaves, spreading them on the ground and serving the food upon them.

Even in fear and uncertainty, the warmth of a meal and the small mercy of keeping our families together felt like a blessing.

After the meal, a soldier approached and said,

We don't have any bedding available tonight. You'll have to manage as best you can. By tomorrow, we'll try to arrange something.

Abbi asked cautiously, how long will we have to stay here? The officer replied, you'll remain here for a day or two. We'll discuss further arrangements in the morning. For now, go and get some rest and allow us to rest too.

That night, those fortunate enough to have blankets spread them out on the cold, hard ground. Those without simply lay on the bare earth.

We fashioned bricks into makeshift pillows. Nazia and Rehan, still very young, had their beloved cushions with them the same ones Grandmother had packed and carried so carefully all this way. They curled up and quickly fell asleep. Nadeem was laid gently on top of a suitcase, covered with a shawl.

The rest of us settled wherever there was space, the cold seeping into our bones.

But Abbi could not sleep. How could he, with the weight of his family's safety on his shoulders? His mind raced through endless worries. The chill in the air was sharp enough to cut through flesh, and anxiety gnawed at everyone's hearts.

What would the morning bring? Would it carry hope or yet another trial?

By God's grace, the night passed in uneasy peace.

By morning, when Abbi awoke, he stepped outside to take in his surroundings. As his eyes adjusted to the new reality, it became clear that this was indeed a military cantonment once a place where soldiers must have lived and drilled.

A row of six or seven large hall-like rooms stood before him. They called them barracks. And this was just one line. Beyond stretched perhaps ten such rows, each containing similar barracks. Between every two barracks lay an open ground, wide and bare. After five barracks stood a vast army kitchen.

Behind the final row was a long stretch of washrooms and bath areas, laid out neatly in lines. Surrounding everything was a high, barbed-wire fence. Even beyond that fence, Abbi noticed another line of barracks separated by yet another double layer of barbed-wire walls.

Armed soldiers patrolled between these fences, pacing watchfully, their weapons always at the ready.

At the corners stood towering watchtowers where more soldiers kept their silent vigil.

Towards the front lay the main gate, heavily guarded. Off to one side, Abbi spotted a canteen it was closed. Beyond that were the officers' offices and a medical clinic, which too was locked.

No matter where he looked, all he could see was barbed wire, cold and merciless, stretching across the horizon, dividing sections and cutting off any thoughts of freedom.

Even beyond the washrooms at the rear of their barracks, another stretch of barbed-wire fencing stood, beyond which lay an enormous ground and faint in the distance a road.

It was not a refugee camp. It was a prison.

By the time morning light had fully embraced the camp, all of us had awakened from what little sleep we had managed to steal. Soon, an officer arrived, his tall frame imposing, yet not unkind.

He summoned all the men, women, and children to gather in the open ground between the barracks.

With him were two others Pandit Ji, a Havildar known for his stern demeanour, and Tiwari Ji, whose role was to oversee inspections.

It was Pandit Ji's task to conduct the falling, the roll call and headcount that they insisted on calling by its military term. Tiwari Ji, meanwhile, was there to inspect to see what people might be carrying.

Pandit Ji, his voice sharp and commanding, began rounding everyone up into lines. The air was chilly, but no one dared to complain.

Once everyone had gathered, he began the count. His tone left no room for hesitation. One by one, families and lone survivors stepped forward as he marked the numbers, ticking them off briskly.

After the count, Pandit Ji and Tiwari Ji began their inspection. But what was there to find?

These were people stripped of everything by war their homes, their livelihoods, and even their identities.

The few belongings they had managed to carry were either necessities or the meager remnants of past lives. There was nothing of value here, except life itself.

After the inspection, the officer motioned for everyone to sit down. On both sides of the barbed wire fence, the war refugees who had arrived with us lowered themselves to the ground.

The officer took a microphone in hand and began to speak, his voice calm yet firm.

I want to share some important information with you all, he said, so there are no misunderstandings, and so you won't need to ask the same questions repeatedly.

A heavy silence fell across the crowd as every ear strained to listen.

First, he continued, you may be here for two months, or it could be two years. Everything depends on when or if the governments of India and Pakistan reach an agreement.

A ripple of uneasy murmurs swept through the crowd.

I ask you all, do not attempt to escape, the officer warned. Certain rules will now apply here. Please do not violate them.

He gestured toward the soldiers stationed around the camp's perimeter.

Some of these guards understand your language. Others do not. Do not argue with them. Do not provoke them. Inside this compound, you will have freedom of movement, and we will provide food rations.

His voice softened slightly.

Children will receive fruits and milk. Whatever rations come to the army will be shared with you. Cooking will be your own responsibility.

He paused to let the information sink in before continuing.

There will be doctors available for basic medical needs. If anyone requires serious treatment, they will be taken to a larger hospital under army supervision.

He raised a finger in emphasis.

Every morning at 7:00 A.M., there will be roll call in front of each barrack. Pandit Ji and Tiwari Ji will take attendance. Bathing and toilet facilities are located at the back. There must be no fighting or quarrelling among yourselves.

A few heads nodded quietly in agreement.

Through the Red Cross, the officer added, each child will receive half a kilogram of milk and every person will get one piece of fruit.

This should begin within a day or two. In addition, each adult will receive a thirty-rupee coupon, which can be used to purchase goods from the camp canteen. The canteen should begin operating within a week.

The officer lowered the microphone. For a moment, the camp was silent no crying children, no anxious whispers. Just a sea of tired, hopeful faces digesting the new reality of their uncertain future.

After outlining the rules, the officer cleared his throat and continued, Now, the most important matter.

A hush fell once again across the gathering.

The medical clinic will be open from 10 A.M. to 12 noon, and again from 4 P.M. to 6 P.M. daily, he announced. Men and women will stay in separate barracks. Every morning, from 10 A.M. to 12 noon, men will be allowed to visit their families.

As soon as he finished, a loud outcry erupted among the people.

No! We won't be separated from our families! one woman shouted.

We don't trust anyone, another man added fiercely. If the men are kept away, there could be abuse or mistreatment of our women.

The murmuring swelled into chaos as fear gripped the hearts of the already traumatized refugees.

No one was willing to accept this new rule. They had already lost so much their homes, their neighbours, their peace. Now, the thought of being parted from loved ones again felt unbearable.

The officer raised his hands, trying to calm the rising panic.

At last, after speaking quietly with some of his aides, he proposed a compromise.

Fine, he said. Each family will stay in a women's barrack, and directly across the wire fence on the other side, the men's barrack will be located. Every morning, families may meet in the women's barrack between10 to 12 P.M.

A wave of relief passed through the crowd. The tension eased.

Some of the younger men, trying to lighten the mood, quickly gave the daily family gathering a nickname Milan Party Time.

The term caught on, and even a few cautious smiles appeared among the weary faces.

Everyone agreed to the new arrangement and began moving back toward their assigned barracks. They gathered their few precious belongings and men spoke earnestly to their wives and daughters, reminding them to always stay together, even when going to the bathrooms. No one trusted strangers here not yet.

After all, they were now officially prisoners of war.

And though they lived with the fragile hope of one day returning to their homeland, fate had taught them not to trust too easily.

They were only beginning this new chapter of life as war refugees and the path ahead was long, shadowed by uncertainty.

Though everyone clung to the hope that one day they would return to their homeland, it was becoming increasingly difficult to believe in fate or promises. Uncertainty hung over their heads like a dark, heavy cloud.

Each barrack, as I've mentioned before, was divided into four or five large halls. Each hall housed eight to ten families.

Not long after everyone had settled in, a few army personnel arrived. They began counting the elderly and small children, scribbling figures into a notebook before quietly disappearing.

An hour later, the elderly and the youngest children were provided with charpoys simple woven cots while the rest of the families received mattresses to lay out on the cold, hard ground.

Despite the hardships, there was something unique about Camp Number 51.

This camp wasn't filled solely with peasants or the uneducated. Here, among the refugees, were doctors, engineers, lawyers, tailors, carpenters, and teachers. Skilled, educated men and women who had once built lives of purpose back in East Pakistan were now gathered here as displaced souls.

The authorities had wisely organized people according to their professional skills and educational levels. In every barrack, a literate woman was appointed as the in-charge, responsible for overseeing the families in her section.

In our barrack, the responsibility fell to Abbi's aunt. She was the most educated woman among us and accepted the duty with quiet dignity.

As for the men's barracks, Abbi, was chosen to be the leader. His calm presence and ability to reassure others had not gone unnoticed.

That day, the army continued providing us with three meals. The food was simple but enough to keep us going.

The next morning brought new developments. Representatives from the Red Cross arrived at the camp accompanied by the officer who had addressed us the day before.

They distributed ration coupons to every family. Each person was allocated 30 rupees worth of coupons to purchase necessities from the camp canteen.

For our family eight members including Abbi, Ammi, Nani, and the children. We received a total of 240 rupees in coupons. Additionally, families with small children were granted another 60 rupees worth of coupons to buy supplies specifically for the little ones.

However, the officer explained that the extra 60 rupees would only be issued for the first month.

Mr. Singh, the officer, also informed everyone that the camp canteen would begin operating in two days. Essentials like toothpaste, toothbrushes, biscuits, custard powder, and other basic items would soon be available.

For the first time in weeks, a sense of fragile order was taking shape.

The army officer soon formed a new committee. He gathered the Pakistani Army Kitchen staff the very men who had once cooked for soldiers and now found themselves displaced like the rest of us and included my Abbi in the group as well.

This team would oversee the camp kitchen, responsible for preparing meals for all the residents. The officer announced that this kitchen group would rotate every three months so that the responsibilities could be shared fairly among the capable men.

The army promptly delivered a full supply of rations to the kitchen, along with all the necessary cooking utensils and equipment.

Meanwhile, the camp canteen was being stocked with utensils, plates, and cooking pots which families could purchase using their ration coupons.

The kitchen group was officially named the "Langar Party." It became the only team permitted to enter the women's section three times a day to cook meals for the camp.

When the large military stoves were not in use by the Langar Party, the women were allowed to cook their own special meals, should they have the ingredients and enough energy left after the day's weariness.

The Langar Party soon became a lifeline for everyone. It was not just about food; it was a reminder that even in a place where freedom was lost and lives had been shattered, cooperation and community could still bring warmth to the cold, uncertain days ahead.

A month slipped by in this new rhythm of survival. But as the days passed, a harsh truth became clear many necessities were still missing.

The sanitation system was insufficient, army doctors were not always available, and a heavier concern weighed on every parent's heart: how long would we remain here? If the stay dragged on, our children's education and futures would surely suffer.

A group of residents, including Abbi, decided to act. They drafted a formal request to the camp commandant, asking for a meeting to discuss these growing concerns.

Soon, the camp authorities arranged a gathering between the camp officer, the Red Cross representatives, and a few selected elders from among us.

In that tense but hopeful meeting, the residents laid out their demands:

Proper sanitation and waste management.

Educational arrangements for the children.

Facilities for tailoring, sewing, and other vocational skills.

Recreational opportunities, including sports and games to keep young minds engaged and spirits lifted.

The Red Cross team listened carefully and promised to consider every request. After a few days, they returned with encouraging news. The camp officer, along with the Red Cross, had agreed that:

Camp residents themselves would be entrusted with organizing and managing many of these services.

We were to nominate qualified people from within our own community. A sense of purpose stirred among us. Abbi and other elders held a camp-wide meeting.

Each family was asked about their skills and past professions. As it turned out, our community was rich in talent despite the hardship.

There were doctors, engineers, electricians, plumbers, carpenters, barbers, and seasoned army kitchen workers.

A list was prepared and sent to the army officer, detailing the names and abilities of the men and women willing to contribute.

Even the youth were included those who had academic training and others skilled in organizing sports like football, cricket, badminton, and carrom board.

In a place designed to strip people of dignity, we had found a way to rebuild a small but meaningful version of society.

Fifteen days later, when the army officer came for his routine inspection of the camp, he called for a general meeting with all the residents.

As always, the first and most desperate question was voiced: When will we be allowed to return home?

And, as always, the officer offered the same vague but hopeful response: Soon we hope to bring you good news.

With that out of the way, the real purpose of the meeting was addressed.

The officer announced that the list of skilled workers previously submitted had been reviewed.

Now, the camp authorities were ready to assign official duties to the volunteers based on their skills and the community's needs.

They also asked the residents to submit a list of any equipment or materials required to carry out their work.

However, no arrangements had yet been made for the children neither for their education nor their general welfare. The officer assured everyone that the matter of schooling and activities for the children would be discussed at the next meeting, and with that, the gathering was dismissed.

Within a day or two, things began to change. The promised responsibilities and supplies were distributed.

One by one, each person stepped into their new role; doctors began organizing a small clinic, barbers set up makeshift stations, tailors gathered materials, and the kitchen group resumed their duties.

The quiet hopelessness that had hung over the camp began to lift ever so slightly. For the first time, people had purpose again.

They were no longer just refugees or war prisoners, they were a community, working together, rebuilding some small sense of normal life amidst the wire fences.

The doctor was assigned to a small dispensary that had been hastily set up within the camp.

A fellow prisoner with medical training was appointed as his assistant and compounder.

The purpose of this makeshift clinic was simple treat minor illnesses and injuries on-site, reducing the need to summon outside doctors. For emergencies, patients would be taken to the nearby Army hospital.

The barber was given a chair and table beneath the shade of a tree, along with the tools of his trade.

The tailor, along with a few women from the camp who were eager seamstresses, received sewing machines and supplies.

The women handled the sewing needs of the women's barracks, while the male tailor set up shop in the men's area. Each person now had their designated corner, their small contribution to this strange, enclosed world.

Those who lacked formal education or specific skills were assigned to cleaning duties.

An educated, older woman was chosen as the warden for each women's barrack.

At the top of this hierarchy stood Abbi's Khala (aunt), who was respected and trusted by everyone.

Likewise, every man's barrack had an educated man as its in-charge.

Abbi not only led his own barrack but was appointed chief supervisor for the entire men's section.

Life settled into a rhythm.

Days began to pass in a way that felt strangely normal as if this prison camp had become its own village, town, or even a nation.

It was as though hope of ever leaving had faded, and the barbed-wire fences marked the boundaries of their world now. The outside world felt distant and unreal.

Each day, at exactly noon, the much-awaited "Milan Party" (Family Meeting Time) took place.

Men and women reunited for two precious hours. Families gathered around their cots, parents playing with their children, sharing stories and laughter amidst the shadows of captivity.

Yet a quiet sorrow lingered.

There were young boys and girls who had no family left their parents lost or killed, left behind or untraceable. They sat silently at the edges, watching others with quiet, longing eyes.

The kitchen team arrived on schedule, carrying large buckets filled with lentils, rice, vegetables, or whatever was available that day.

The Army's massive langar kitchen stood on the women's side of the camp, and after cooking, the boys from the kitchen group distributed meals barrack by barrack, counting portions carefully according to family size.

Rice, dal, potatoes, chapatis sometimes even an egg if supplies allowed.

Though they were prisoners, they had created a semblance of community.

Yet deep inside, everyone knew this was not life. It was simply survival.

Need and hardship are strange things they reveal a person's true character. They also test the loyalty and bonds of family and kin.

A situation arose that made this painfully clear.

One day, the camp officer distributed ceiling fans to each barrack to help with the sweltering heat.

In the large room where we children stayed, four fans were allotted. Naturally, they were meant to be installed where the children and the elderly slept.

But human nature is not always fair. The woman in charge of our barrack the appointed "In charge Madam" had different ideas.

She directed one fan to be fixed above her own bed, another above her favoured family: a doctor's household. The remaining two? They were placed above the beds of her closest allies and flatterers.

The children, the sick, and the elderly were left to swelter in the heat.

When the army officer arrived for an inspection, he noticed the arrangement immediately. His face darkened with disapproval.

Madam, he said firmly, the fans were provided for the children and the elderly. You will either move the people or the fans to make sure they benefit those who need them most.

But troubles in the camp weren't just born of hardship sometimes, human nature itself made things harder.

Some of the women often quarrelled, especially over food. Their main grievance? That mother with children received slightly more food sometimes an extra potato or an egg.

This became a regular issue for Ammi. Since Abbi was one of the kitchen supervisors, and the Pashtun men working there were fond of us children Nadeem, Rehan, and Nazia; they often served a little extra on our plates.

Because we were the youngest in the camp, we also received more milk. If any milk remained at the end of the day, Ammi would carefully make kheer, a sweet rice pudding, to keep us nourished.

But inevitably, the murmurs and taunts would follow. The more educated women, surprisingly, would join the less literate ones in throwing barbed comments at Ammi.

Of course, the lady of the kitchen supervisor gets special treatment. Her children eat like kings while the rest of us starve!

Ammi usually smiled and let the remarks slide off her like water from a duck's back. But sometimes, I saw the sadness in her eyes.

It was as if some women had resigned themselves to this prison, this camp life, accepting it as permanent and forgetting the world outside. They had given up hope of ever being free.

Yet, despite all this, there was one beautiful truth. Inside these fences, among these prisoners of war, there was unity. Punjabis, Biharis, people from Uttar Pradesh, all lived together, not as separate communities, but as one people.

We all shared the same sorrows. And deep down, every heart longed for the same thing, to return home. To return to our loved ones.

The camp canteen had finally begun functioning smoothly.

The women would place special requests with the canteen staff for food and other necessities, and once those items arrived, the staff would call them over to collect their goods in exchange for coupons.

Before long, the canteen was also well-stocked with utensils. Everyone purchased their own, and now meals were eaten from personal plates and bowls a small return to normalcy.

Between every two barracks stood a common water tap. Women would gather there to wash their utensils and collect drinking water.

In the beginning, they would form long lines, often quarrelling over their turns. But, over time, everyone began to understand;

The tap wasn't going anywhere. The water wouldn't stop flowing. Whoever needed water would get their share eventually.

Of course, bathrooms were a different story. People, eager to bathe first, would claim the taps by tying clothes or scarves around them a silent declaration of territory.

This problem was far worse in the women's section, where basic human nature greed, impatience, and selfishness would occasionally rear its head.

And just like that, three more months slipped by.

One day, an army officer arrived at the camp accompanied by several members of the Red Cross.

He addressed all of us gathered there. What do you need? What supplies are you short of?

Though they had consistently brought various items for the women, children, and the rest of us, the officer still asked the question giving us a chance to voice any specific concerns.

As always, Abbi stepped forward.

But instead of listing supplies, he asked the question that weighed heaviest on everyone's mind:

We would like to know, first and foremost. How much longer will we be here?

The officer sighed.

We still have no information, he replied, his voice patient but firm. As soon as we receive any news or updates, you will be the first to know. But until that day comes, looking after your well-being remains our responsibility.

He paused. So, please tell us what else you need. We'll do our best to provide it.

Abbi nodded and spoke for all the families.

We feel completely cut off from the outside world. If we could be given a radio, it would remind us that we are still a part of it still connected to life beyond these fences.

He continued, Also, we've asked before, but it's vital

Arrangements must be made for the children's education.

The younger ones need toys and play equipment.

And the educated young men and women, especially those without families, should be given work or responsibilities so they too feel they have a place and a purpose.

The Red Cross representatives listened carefully, taking down notes as Abbi spoke. Finally, they promised:

The Red Cross team will return next week with solutions to all these issues.

The very next morning, the entire camp awoke to a surprise no one could have imagined.

Each day, a loudspeaker mounted in the camp would blare out instructions mostly to summon people for the daily roll call.

But that morning, after the usual headcount, as everyone returned to their chores, suddenly through the loudspeaker came the melodious strains of Binaca Geet Mala.

Beautiful, nostalgic songs from back home floated through the camp.

A ripple of surprise swept across the crowd. Children, young boys, and girls burst into joyful laughter. Some even began to dance.

It felt as though spring had arrived in a place where only fear had reigned.

And why not? For those who had been living in constant dread, this music was a reminder of life itself and the fragile hope of a future.

Then came the news broadcast. For the first time in months, people heard what was happening in the outside world.

From that day onward, it became a routine. Every morning, the loudspeakers would play two hours of songs and news. In the evenings, there would be another hour of updates.

Slowly, amidst the bleak routine of imprisonment, life began to feel a little more normal. They say music is food for the soul.

In those moments, our worries and sorrows dissolved into the rhythm of the songs, while the news kept us connected to a world we feared had forgotten us.

A week later, the Red Cross team returned, this time bringing solutions to many of the problems that had plagued us especially those concerning the children and the idle youth.

It was decided that the young men and women in the camp who were educated would take on the responsibility of teaching the children.

The Red Cross provided large tarpaulins to serve as classrooms, blackboards, and a generous supply of notebooks, pencils, and other essentials.

The educated young women were assigned roles based on their qualifications, and the children were divided into classes according to age. Each class was given its own teacher.

On the men's side of the camp, young men taught the boys, while on the women's side, young women taught the younger children and the girls.

Some young men were even given responsibilities by the army authorities, helping with the prisoners' records and other administrative tasks.

And so, at last, a school was born within the camp.

The Red Cross also supplied sports equipment like footballs, basketballs, and cricket gear.

For indoor play, they provided carrom boards and Ludo sets.

Those youths who had shown talent in sports were appointed as instructors.

Soon, a new rhythm took hold of our lives. Each morning, from 9 A.M. to noon, classes were held.

In the evenings, the children played under the guidance of their new coaches.

It was as if life had been rekindled behind the barbed wire fences. The prisoners, once desperate and fearful, had begun to accept the uncertainty of their fate.

Whatever comes, we will face it together, they told each other. God is watching over us.

The women, too, had found solace in their own world. Some busied themselves preparing pickles, while others devoted their time to sewing and embroidery. A few young women learned handicrafts, while others took lessons in cooking.

Ammi spent part of her day teaching knitting to the younger girls.

Slowly, the prison camp had transformed into a village of its own, a community born out of shared suffering.

In the afternoons and at night, when the langar's great cooking fires died down, the women would slip in to toast their breads to a crisp, or if they had managed to save any milk, they would prepare custard or kheer.

Even luxury had taken on a humble face in this place.

Pandit Ji and Tiwari Ji, the guards who patrolled between the barbed wire fences, became an unexpected link between families.

At the women's polite requests, they would carry dishes sweet puddings, halwa, or simple cooked meals across the barrier to waiting husbands, brothers, or sons on the men's side.

Our job is to keep watch, not to run your kitchen, they would scold playfully, pretending irritation.

But soon Pandit Ji would be peering curiously through the fence, teasing, we don't usually eat food cooked by strangers. But seeing your pickled vegetables reminds me of my wife's cooking back home.

Then, in a softer tone, he would ask with a grin, any chance I could have a little of that pickle?

It was a strange, bittersweet world where prisoners and their guards shared the same human emotions. Their pain had become a common bond.

A few days later, the Army officer brought exciting news:

A special gift has arrived from the world of cinema.

The film Pakeezah would be screened for the prisoners of war. It had been sent especially for us and would be shown on Saturday night. After that, they announced, other films would follow, though each would require a coupon worth 25 paise.

The announcement caused a wave of joy throughout the camp. At least once a month, we'll have a little entertainment. Everyone began looking forward to Saturday.

On the big day, the women hurriedly finished all their chores before sunset. The children, too, wrapped up their games and duties.

As dusk settled, the back of the camp a large open ground surrounded by barbed wire fences was transformed into a makeshift cinema.

Two tall bamboo poles held up large white sheets that served as screens. A projector was set up, reels ready to roll.

At last, permission was given for the prisoners and their families to gather.

They streamed into the field, spreading blankets on the ground. The air buzzed with anticipation.

As soon as the first images flickered onto the screen, the audience erupted into applause.

From the nearby road, curious passersby peered through the wire, trying to understand who these people were and what was happening behind the fenced-off area a place where no outsiders ever came.

That night, armed soldiers stood alert along every edge of the field.

But inside the fence, we had forgotten all fear. We were engrossed in "Pakeezah".

Some of the younger men, caught up in the joy of the songs, even began dancing, only to be gently scolded and told to sit down so those behind them could see.

By the time the film ended and we returned to our barracks, it felt as though, for a few precious hours, we had been freed if only in spirit.

The next morning, as the soldiers packed up the projector and equipment, they told the children,

Some film negatives have fallen if you want them, you can pick them up. Eagerly, Nadeem and I began gathering the small, broken strips of film. While collecting the pieces, we wandered along the edge of the barbed wire fence.

A man passing by on the road outside noticed us and asked curiously,

What are you children doing inside the army camp?

Without thinking, I replied, we are prisoners.

Before I could say another word, an army guard hurried over.

He quickly moved us children back inside the fence and sternly told the bystanders to clear the area immediately.

Later that morning, during his usual round, the Army Officer arrived.

So, how did you enjoy the film? he asked with a smile.

It was wonderful! everyone responded enthusiastically.

The officer nodded and then made an announcement.

From now on, for everyone's safety, films will be shown separately one day for the women's camp and another for the men's camp. No one is allowed to enter the rear ground anymore.

Such small joys made a world of difference in those difficult days.

After that, Abbi approached the Army Officer with a request.

Ramadan is approaching. Could you please arrange for us to have the call to prayer (Adhan)? Also, we need to plan how to manage Suhoor and Iftar.

The officer listened carefully and replied,

Since you are the kitchen in-charge, discuss the arrangements with the others and let me know what you need. We'll organize everything accordingly. We'll also provide the prayer times for Meerut, and at every Adhan time, a siren will sound.

The community asked if they could pray in congregation. The officer granted permission but added,

You may hold congregational prayers, but only within your own barracks. And there should be no unnecessary gatherings or discussions beyond the prayers.

Soon, everyone busied themselves preparing for Ramadan.

Meanwhile, Abbi received a letter a rare and precious thing in those days. It came from an old friend and colleague, Bashir Haris, who had worked alongside him at PIA (Pakistan International Airlines).

Mr. Bashir had sent the letter through Mr. H.R. Naqi, the Chief Engineer at PIA, hoping to find out whether we were alive and where we had ended up after the chaos.

The letter had travelled all the way from Karachi and had undergone strict scrutiny before it was finally handed to Abbi. The authorities allowed him to reply but only to confirm that he was alive and well.

Every word of the letter would be checked before it was sent out, for security reasons. The primary purpose of this correspondence was to give families the comfort of knowing that their loved ones had survived.

In that camp, even a simple letter felt like a bridge between two worlds the imprisoned and the free.

Meanwhile, back home, our grandfather, Dr. Shams-uz-Zaman Khan, had been relentlessly searching for news of us. Since our uncle, Naseem Khan, was involved in politics at the time, he had valuable contacts and connections.

From Patna, Ammi's uncle, Dr. Idris Khan of Ismail Manzil (who was also our maternal grandfather), joined the efforts to gather any information about our whereabouts and condition.

Some of our relatives had managed to escape and reach Pakistan, but none of them could trace us. It was as if we had vanished into thin air.

One day, my grandfather mentioned our disappearance to Master Sahib (*Lakhan* Singh) who had once taught Abbi and remained a family friend. Master Sahib asked his son, the same army officer who had once brought my grandfather's letter to Abbi at the Dhaka camp. His son replied,

The civilians from the Dhaka camp were taken as prisoners of war. I will find out where they've been sent.

After some time, Lakhan Singh's son was able to confirm the news to Uncle Naseem Khan:

Yes, they are alive. Some civilians are being held at the POW camp in Meerut.

When this news finally reached our family, my grandfather, Dr. Shams-uz-Zaman Khan, immediately travelled from Birnawa to Patna.

He and Uncle Naseem gathered ₹6000 and arranged a parcel of food and supplies.

Dr. Idris Khan (Ammi Uncle) sent clothing and other necessities for us and the children.

Uncle Naseem Khan secured special permission to visit the camp. Though he was not allowed to meet us directly, he and Abbi were able to glimpse each other from a distance across the barbed wire fence that separated the prisoners from the outside world.

The army officials assured Uncle Naseem that the money and supplies would be delivered safely. Abbi was called into the office, where he received the gifts and counted the money. He was asked to sign a receipt and confirm in writing that our family was alive and well.

The cash was not handed over directly; instead, vouchers worth ₹6000 were issued. These would be distributed to Abbi in monthly instalments of ₹500, which could be used at the camp's canteen.

Even in captivity, across countries and borders, the love and concern of family found a way to reach us, piercing through barbed wire and despair.

A few days later, Ramadan began, and with it, the entire camp's routine changed. Mothers who had young children would prepare a little extra food for them to keep for suhoor.

From the camp kitchen, prisoners were given two pooris and a cup of tea to start their fast. Those who had vouchers could purchase dry goods like fruits and biscuits from the canteen to supplement their meals.

For iftar, the kitchen provided chana dal and roti. If the women wanted to prepare something special, they would send the ingredients across the barbed wire fence to their husbands or sons through Tiwari J*i* or whichever soldier happened to be on duty at the time.

Tiwari Ji, or another soldier patrolling between the fences, often helped pass food and supplies between the men's and women's quarters.

After breaking their fast, the prisoners performed congregational prayers in the verandas of their respective barracks.

Ramadan passed peacefully. There was no worry about sewing new Eid clothes or collecting Eidi for the children. The only sounds that punctuated the days were announcements over the loudspeaker:

The daily news, and the sirens signalling the times for suhoor and iftar. One of the children from the camp had been chosen to call the adhan.

The most challenging part of Ramadan was lining up at 7 A.M. for the daily falling the headcount. But even that was a necessity. Rumour's often spread that prisoners from nearby camps had attempted to escape and were caught.

There was another camp near ours, separated by four or five layers of barbed wire. We could see the prisoners moving in the distance, but they were too far away to speak with.

We never knew if they were civilians like us or captured soldiers. Occasionally, we heard shouting or disturbances from their side, but after some time, even their camp settled into a routine similar to ours.

Ramadan was passing not in the warmth of home, but behind barbed wires, in a world where survival had become both an act of endurance and of faith.

As Ramadan drew to a close and Eid approached, a new worry settled over the camp. How would they celebrate Eid?

There were no relatives nearby, no homes to return to. Yet hope, like the human spirit, refused to wither.

The prisoners sent a letter to the army officer, requesting permission to celebrate Eid in some small way perhaps even just to watch a film together. They waited anxiously for a reply, but none came.

Then, on Chaand Raat the night when the new moon was sighted, news swept through the camp like a warm breeze. On Eid day, qawwals would be visiting to perform for the prisoners.

As soon as the crescent moon was spotted, a spontaneous burst of joy rippled through the camp. The men overturned empty cauldrons and began beating them like drums.

The clanging sounds rang out, not as noise but as a declaration, we are still alive, we can still celebrate. But the real surprise came on Eid morning.

Word spread that some of the influential families of Meerut had learned about the civilians held in Camp 51, and that this would be their first Eid in captivity.

With special permission, they had arranged for massive cauldrons of biryani and kheer to be sent to the prisoners.

Before the food reached them, it was thoroughly checked by the authorities for the prisoners' safety. Only after this inspection was it distributed among the families.

When the biryani and kheer were finally served, it was as though Eid's joy had doubled. The rich aroma of the food filled the air and lifted spirits.

All day long, people talked of nothing else but the feast. That evening, the entire camp eagerly prepared for the arrival of the qawwals, ready to embrace a moment of festivity after so many months of sorrow.

A celebration of survival, resilience, and the hope that someday, Eid would once again be spent in freedom, among loved ones.

Around 8 P.M., the qawwali singers arrived. The event was arranged in the men's camp, in the open ground between the barracks.

On the other side of the barbed wire fence, women gathered in their section to listen and catch a glimpse of the performers.

As the qawwali began, a wave of joy spread through the prisoners. People swayed gently to the rhythm, savouring the rare moment of celebration.

But when the qawwals launched into "Dama Dam Mast Qalandar," something extraordinary happened. A spiritual frenzy overtook the crowd.

Some listeners, overcome with emotion, began to sway violently, their bodies moving as if possessed by an ancient ecstasy.

A commotion broke out. The soldiers standing guard didn't understand what was happening and rushed forward, thinking perhaps a riot or a dangerous outburst had begun. They started grabbing at the men in a panic.

The crowd tried to explain amidst the confusion. This is not a disturbance, they pleaded. It's a spiritual trance. The music, it takes hold of people.

For a moment, the performance was paused while the misunderstanding was sorted out. Once the guards understood, they stepped back, though they kept a cautious watch.

The qawwali resumed.

The music flowed deep into the night, carrying with it the bittersweet blend of sorrow and hope that had become the prisoners' constant companion.

Midnight came and went in a chorus of voices lifted in celebration of the first Eid they had spent behind barbed wire, yet somehow, still together.

The next day, as if the universe wished to grant them yet another taste of freedom, the film *"Anarkali"* was screened for the prisoners.

It was a gift from the film community, a brief but welcome escape into a world of romance and history, far from the harsh reality of their captivity.

And so, Ramadan and Eid passed not in their homes, not with all their loved ones, but embraced by a community of survivors. Even as prisoners, they found ways to celebrate life.

Among the young men imprisoned in the camp, those who had no family left, a tight-knit group had formed.

They were mostly between sixteen and twenty-five years old.

The leader of their little gang was a spirited youth named Arif. Mischief was his second nature. He was always on the lookout for new ways to tease Pandit Ji and Tiwari Ji, the soldiers who supervised our daily counts, and to stir up harmless trouble.

Arif and his gang found solace in their antics. Teaching the younger children's pranks, pulling off little stunts, these had become their way of forgetting the sorrows that otherwise threatened to overwhelm them.

Their mischief brought both frustration and laughter to the camp.

One morning, during the usual headcount, Tiwari Ji noticed something amiss. Two boys from Arif's group were missing.

Where are they? he demanded. Go check the bathrooms!

Arif and a few of his friends went off to search. They soon returned.

Sir, they're not there. They went to the clinic last night and never came back.

It was now well past 7:00 A.M., and the two boys were nowhere to be found. The others remained standing in the morning line, worried and restless.

Since the clinic was near the camp's outer boundary, fear spread quickly; had they tried to escape?

Just as the tension was reaching its peak, a strange noise came from the corner of the yard a dull thudding, as if someone was knocking from inside a drum.

The soldiers rushed over and overturned two large, upside-down cooking cauldrons. Out tumbled the missing boys, gasping for air, dishevelled and drenched in sweat.

As soon as they were given water and could speak, one boy turned to Arif and scolded him,

You said we only had to hide for five minutes!

A ripple of laughter spread through Arif's gang and even some of the children watching the scene. But Tiwari Ji was not amused. His face darkened with anger.

Because of your foolishness, we've kept everyone standing in this heat for over half an hour. And what if these two had suffocated and died?

As punishment, Tiwari Ji ordered Arif and his closest friends to stand on one leg in the blazing sun for three hours. Afterward, he warned them sternly,

If you pull another stunt like this, the consequences will be far worse.

The boys apologized humbly and promised to behave. But, of course, no one truly believed that they would. Mischief was the only comfort they had left.

Life in the camp had settled into a familiar rhythm. Every morning began with the same routine the falling the daily headcount followed by music blaring from the loudspeakers and then the news bulletin.

By nine o'clock, the children gathered at their makeshift schoolrooms. Each class met under tarpaulins spread out on the verandas of the barracks.

Classes continued until noon, followed by the cherished "Milan Party" hour when families reunited.

In the evenings, the children gathered again, this time for sports under the guidance of the appointed coach.

Abbi, always keen on building morale, had organized a football team. Every week, a match was held, Abbi's team against a team from another barrack.

They had also formed two cricket teams, with matches taking place on Sundays.

In his younger days, Abbi had been an accomplished football player, representing both his college and the Patna

Electric Department's team. Naturally, he took charge of coaching our football team and proudly captained it.

On match days, the entire camp buzzed with excitement. Whenever a team won, their supporters would flip over the large cooking cauldrons and beat them like drums with oversized ladles.

From across the barbed wire fence, the women and children would clap and cheer. These small joys were the light that brightened the heavy shadows of captivity.

The Red Cross continued to visit, regularly bringing toys, books, and other supplies for the children. The Indian Army personnel also seemed to soften toward us.

Over time, their treatment grew kinder, and it no longer felt as though we were prisoners of war. It felt instead like a village, a community with its own rules, its own routines, and its own fragile, hard-earned harmony.

The soldiers, too, were far from home and family. In each child, they saw their own sons and daughters. In every mother and sister, they recognized their own loved ones.

This, perhaps, was the truest form of humanity, the invisible bond that quietly connected all of us.

If we were bound by the chains of captivity, they too were bound by the chains of duty. And so, in this strange world fenced by barbed wire, we all endured together.

Then came our first *Bakra Eid*; Eid al-Adha. But it felt hollow, subdued. People gathered in quiet groups, wondering how to observe the festival.

There would be no sacrifice this year. Meat was out of the question inside a prison camp.

But once again, the people of Meerut showed their generosity and compassion. They obtained special permission from the authorities, arranged for a goat to be sacrificed, and sent the meat into the camp, after it passed through rigorous inspection.

That *Bakra Eid* turned out to be almost joyful, in its own way.
The only difference from past years was that after the Eid prayers and again after the *Bakra Eid* prayers, men and women embraced each other and wept quietly.

They cried not only out of longing for loved ones left behind, but out of fear for what the future still held.

As a small gift to us, the camp authorities arranged a special screening of the film *Aadmi*. A movie was shown every month anyway, but on Eid, *Bakra Eid*, and India's Independence Day, they waived the usual 25-paise coupon fee.

The generous citizens of Meerut had also arranged something else, every few months, they would send in a goat for the camp. It added a rare luxury to our meals and lifted everyone's spirits especially the children.

Whenever the young men arrived carrying the food, the children would giggle and cry out, Boṭī! Give us the meat! Leave the bones for our mother.

Such were the small, precious joys of life behind barbed wire.

But despite these comforts, fear still lingered in our hearts and in the hearts of the soldiers guarding us. The camp authorities feared a breakout or some accident, especially at night.

If a woman or child needed to use the latrines after dark, it was always a challenge. The toilets were located far away, beyond all the barracks, across the open ground at the far end of the camp.

So, the women and children formed small groups for safety. The soldiers in the watchtowers would shine their flashlights to keep an eye on them.

If it was especially late, the guards would call down, where are you going? and shine the torch again as they returned.

They would not lower their lights until every person had safely re-entered the barracks. Only then would the guards relax.

Several women in the camp gave birth during those long, uncertain months. For deliveries, they were taken to the army hospital outside the camp.

The women who still possessed a few small pieces of jewellery, hidden and preserved through the chaos, often sold them quietly.

With the little money they managed to gather, they would send the nurses to purchase baby supplies and other essentials from outside.

Camp-issued tokens were useless beyond the barbed wire. Even when family members managed to send money through money orders, the funds were only given to them in the form of those same in-camp tokens.

The world outside remained distant, unreachable even when new life was born within the walls of captivity.

We even observed *Muharram* inside the camp.

Our Shia brothers, who were among the detainees, requested permission to hold majlis and Matam.

A similar request came from the neighbouring camp, where the numbers were few but the devotion ran deep.

Permission was granted to both groups. However, things soon spiralled out of control.

The mourners in the other camp began performing Matam using blades. As the self-inflicted wounds began to bleed and the intensity of the ritual grew, the scene became chaotic. Blood flowed freely.

The army immediately surrounded the area and ordered the ritual to stop at once. Tension gripped the camp like a vice. Soldiers cocked their rifles and forced everyone to their knees.

In our camp, the Matam had not yet begun. But the escalating situation next door led the officers to halt all mourning rituals across both camps.

The injured were rushed to the hospital, and as punishment, all previously granted privileges were revoked from the other camp.

Despite many appeals from the detainees, the officers were firm.

You should have informed us in advance, the army commander declared. Why were blades even used?

For two or three days, the tension hung heavy in the air like a storm cloud.

Then, the commanding officer called a meeting in our camp.

Before it began, everyone's belongings were thoroughly searched.

At the gathering, the officer addressed us gravely. If anything like this happens here, he warned, we will shut everything down.

Your security is our top priority.

If even one person dies inside this camp, we will be answerable at many levels. This is your final warning do not engage in any actions that could endanger yourselves or others.

The atmosphere was already tense. Everyone was still mentally shaken from the recent events, when Arif and his group of boys stirred up fresh trouble.

The very next morning, as Pandit Ji arrived for the daily falling (headcount), four boys were missing.

By 7 A.M., the rest of us stood lined up. No one was allowed to move until the missing boys were found.

Search parties combed every corner from the bathrooms to the clinic.

Even the empty kitchen cauldrons were turned upside down, but there was no sign of them.

Each barrack's roof was supported by large wooden beams, and every so often, the eerie cries of crows or sparrows echoed from above.

At times, even the howls of stray dogs and cats punctuated the heavy silence.

An hour passed. The children began crying from fatigue, but the four boys remained missing.

Pandit Ji and Tiwari Ji were seething with anger.

Suddenly, one of the detainees spoke up from the line, Sir, perhaps you should check the rooftops too. Some of us need to use the restroom our stomachs are hurting.

Pandit Ji barked an order. Search the roofs and the trees nearby!

Five minutes later, the missing boys were found hauled down from two of the barracks' rooftops, looking sheepish and dishevelled.

That day, the entire camp's frustration exploded toward these boys.

Pandit Ji and Tiwari Ji were beside themselves with fury, and many feared the boys might receive a severe beating. Yet, as tempers flared, others urged leniency.

After much discussion, it was decided they would be punished made to stand for hours in the blazing sun and sternly warned next time, they would be confined in isolation.

Abbi and others, however, felt a pang of sympathy. Everyone understood why the boys kept acting out.

In a crowd of thousands, they just wanted to remind the world that they existed too forgotten souls who had lost their families, desperately seeking attention in whatever childish ways they could.

In our camp, there was a man whose real name no one quite remembered the boys had nicknamed him *Makhan* (butter).

His wife had been killed during the war. He had barely managed to escape with his two young daughters. Since men and women were housed separately in the camp, his little girls had been placed in the women's barracks.

There, a young woman named Razia, somewhere between twenty and twenty-five years old, took the two girls under her wing. She, too, had lost her entire family in the bloodshed and was now alone.

Razia kept the girls close at all times, like a protective mother hen. Every evening, when families gathered at the wire fences to speak to each other, Makhan's daughters would stand by the barrier, calling to their father, while Razia stood beside them.

She would chat with Makhan Sahib about the girls, sharing their little troubles and joys.

But Arif and his gang of mischievous boys would often poke fun. As they passed by, they tossed teasing comments, making up exaggerated tales about Makhan and Razia.

They've buttered up to each other now, they'd snicker. See? The bread has found its butter!

The poor man was mortified by their constant teasing.

Abbi frequently tried to reason with the boys, but they were not ones to be easily tamed.

This prison camp was an odd, bittersweet world. Everyone was simply passing the time in whatever way they could surviving, coping, enduring.

At first, Makhan Sahib was embarrassed and angry about the jokes.

But gradually, even he began to see Razia not as a stranger or a burden, but as a gentle mother figure for his girls perhaps, even as a companion in the life they had been forced to build behind barbed wire.

Life in the camp continued in its bittersweet rhythm until August arrived the month of *freedom.*

Independence Day but a complicated one. Two countries, two dates, side by side, August 14 and August 15.

A few prisoners submitted a request to celebrate August 14, but it was quickly deemed impossible. The guards feared it might stir tensions.

Restlessness began to brew among the prisoners. Thoughts of home gnawed at them. The weight of captivity felt heavier. Murmurs rippled through the camp: When will we finally go back?

The barrack leaders were summoned. They were firmly told to discourage such discussions.

Until both governments; India and Pakistan, come to an agreement, no one is leaving. And as for Independence Day, the officer added, you may celebrate it, but only on August 15.

As for August 14, discuss among yourselves and propose something reasonable.

Abbi and the other leaders asked for a day to consider. They gathered the prisoners and opened the floor to suggestions.

Everyone fell into deep thought. Tensions were high. It was clear they needed a solution that would keep people's minds and hearts occupied.

After a long pause, Abbi shared an idea. Why don't we hold a Sports Week? he proposed.

For the entire week leading up to August 15, we can host tournaments and games. That way, everyone stays busy, spirits stay high, and we avoid any conflict.

The others nodded in agreement. It was a perfect plan active, harmless, and unifying.

Abbi presented the idea to the army officer. Both he and the other officials welcomed it warmly. Sometimes, a simple idea could ease heavy hearts.

The very next day, an official announcement echoed through the camp loudspeaker

From August 8 to August 14, we will celebrate Sports Week

The teachers were instructed to prepare the children for various games and competitions according to their age groups.

The older boys were told that for three days and three nights, cricket and football matches would be held.

The winners' names would be announced on August 14, and prizes would be awarded on August 15.

In preparation for the celebrations, children were also taught poems to recite. Someone had specially requested Allama Iqbal's Bang-e-Dra to be brought into the camp.

I, too, was given a poem to memorize and perform. My teacher had chosen "The Bird's Lament." I was to recite it before the camp's army in-charge and other officers on August 15.

Semi Appa (my elder sister) signed up for the sack race, and Nadeem entered the sprint.

As for little Rehan and Nazia, they were too young to compete in anything. But they clapped with all their might, sitting beside Nani, their grandmother, cheering for all of us.

The camp, which had so long echoed only with the sounds of counting drills and urgent commands, now rang with laughter, shouts of excitement, and the hopeful spirit of a people who refused to let their dreams be caged.

A wave of excitement had swept over the camp. Each day, after school, the children eagerly threw themselves into games and competitions.

Every kind of sport was being prepared for children of all ages.

The young and old alike were determined to win.

Finally, August 8 arrived the much-awaited Sports Week had begun.

Every afternoon, competitions filled three to four hours with energy and enthusiasm. The contests were fierce.

The names of the winners were carefully recorded. As for those who lost, they were gently reminded:

Winning and losing are both parts of the game. Today they won tomorrow, it might be you.

The little girls were busy preparing for the upcoming Independence Day event. They practiced their tableaus and memorized their poems.

Meanwhile, the three-day cricket match was held. Arif's team claimed victory though the losing side whispered that the umpire had been unfair.

In the football tournament, Abbi's team triumphed.

The grown-ups waited eagerly for the 14th, when the final results would be announced.

The children, meanwhile, dreamed of the prizes they hoped to receive.

At last, August 14 dawned. That entire day was spent preparing for the evening's celebration.

As the sun began to set, the names of the winners in each event were announced excluding, of course, the team sports like football and cricket.

Winners were shown how to stand proudly on the 1st, 2nd, and 3rd place podiums and taught how to bow slightly to receive their awards.

Afterward, Balushahi, a sweet pastry, was distributed to everyone.

You all celebrated the week so beautifully, the officer announced. Let us sweeten our mouths in honor of your efforts.

By the evening of the 14th, the entire camp had been decorated. Small tricolour flags fluttered everywhere.

The Trianga was proudly displayed across every barrack and fence.

Preparations for August 15 were in full swing. The Red Cross had arranged prizes and gifts for the sports winners.

The plan was set. After the morning falling (roll call) at 7 A.M., the flag hoisting would take place, followed by performances prepared by the children.

Everyone was told to sleep early so they could rise at dawn for the big day.

The camp buzzed with joy finally, a day to look forward to. Everyone quickly finished their tasks and prepared for sleep, their hearts light and full of anticipation.

On the morning of August 15, everyone was up at dawn. It seemed as if the children had not slept at all.

At 7:00 A.M., Tiwari Ji and Pandit Ji arrived. Everyone lined up in front of their barracks. Roll call falling began. One by one, the residents of each barrack were counted.

Once the roll call was complete, the entire camp gathered in the large ground where the sports competitions had been held. A table was set up for the Army Officer.

Women and children gathered on the women's side of the ground, while the arrangements for the men and boys were made on the opposite side.

Prizes for the winners were placed neatly on tables on both sides. The women oversaw the children's awards, while the men managed the arrangements for the older boys and men.

When all the preparations were finally complete and everyone was seated in their designated spots, the Army suddenly went on high alert.

For the first time, we saw a helicopter land up close. It descended slowly and touched down on the ground nearby.

Along with the Army Officer, a senior official stepped out of the helicopter.

The children, their eyes wide with wonder, jumped up and down in excitement, treating the helicopter as if it were some grand spectacles. The mothers hurried to hold them back.

The loudspeakers crackled to life, announcing the flag hoisting ceremony. Everyone stood in unison.

The guest of honour approached the flagpole, and with a firm tug, the Indian flag soared into the sky.

As the flag unfurled, the national anthem began to play over the loudspeakers. The music echoed across the camp, stirring feelings of both pride and longing in every heart.

Once the anthem concluded, one of the teachers stepped up to the microphone and officially began the day's program.

People on both sides of the camp waited eagerly for the children's performances to begin.

The young girls opened the program with Allama Iqbal's patriotic anthem,

Sāre Jahān se Achchā Hindostān Hamārā.

Next came various tableaux set to different poems. Among them was Ismail Meeruthi's famous children's poem,

rab kā shukr adā kar bhaa.ī
jis ne hamārī gaay banā.ī

"Thank the Lord, my brother / Who made our gentle cow.

I, meanwhile, sat waiting nervously for my turn. Abbi watched me closely, eager to see if my voice could carry the emotion, he hoped for to move the hearts of the Army Officer and the guest of honour for whom I had been specially prepared. Finally, my moment arrived.

I stepped forward and, in my best voice, began singing *Allama Iqbal's* deeply emotional poem Parindey ki Faryaad (The Bird's Lament)

aatā hai yaad mujh ko guzrā huā zamāna
vo baaġh kī bahāreñ vo sab kā chahchahānā
āzādiyāñ kahāñ vo ab apne ghoñsle kī
apnī ḳhushī se aanā apnī ḳhushī se jaanā

I remember the days now gone,
The gardens in spring, the songs of everyone.

No longer can I return to my little nest,
To come and go as I once loved best.

As my voice echoed through the loudspeakers, a hush fell over the entire camp.

A stillness, profound and heavy. Faces, young and old, were wet with tears. Even the guest of honour had tears glistening in his eyes.

I continued, unaware of the waves I was stirring in the hearts around me:

kyā bad-nasīb huuñ maiñ ghar ko taras rahā huuñ
sāthī to haiñ vatan meñ maiñ qaid meñ paḌā huuñ

What misfortune is mine, longing for home,
My friends live free while in prison I roam.

At those lines, many in the crowd broke into sobs. People wept openly

I sang on, not fully grasping the meaning of the words, but feeling their weight in the air around me. As I reached the final Vers.

gaanā ise samajh kar ḳhush hoñ na sunñe vale
dukhte hue diloñ kī fariyād ye sadā hai
āzād mujh ko kar de o qaid karne vale
maiñ be-zabāñ huuñ qaidī tū chhoḌ kar duā le

Sing not this song with joy, O listener dear,
These are cries from hearts that bleed and fear.
Set me free, O captor, my silent plea,
I am voiceless release me, and take my prayer with thee.

The Army Officer suddenly rose from his chair. He came forward, lifted me into his arms, tears streaming down his face.

My child, he said, his voice trembling, we are helpless and bound too. But one day, you will all return home. One day, you will play once again in your courtyard. And perhaps, I too will finally sleep in peace beneath my roof.

Then, trying to smile through his emotion, he turned to my teacher and said teasingly, so *this* is why you requested Iqbal's book to make us all cry.

After the emotional performances, the teacher turned to the Army Officer and asked,

Sir, out of all today's performances, which did you think was the best? Who should receive first, second, and third place?

The Officer smiled and replied,

You teachers should decide that yourselves. But as for me, He paused, his eyes turning towards me.

I want to give this little girl a special prize from my side.

He reached into the gifts he had brought along for the children and took out a magic slate. Handing it to me, he said warmly,

Start writing, child. One day, you will write this story too.

I didn't fully grasp the weight of his words at the time. But the slate oh, the slate I never forgot.

Even after freedom came, and long after the camp days were over, that slate remained with me, a cherished memory of hope born in captivity.

What a beautiful moment so symbolic.

As he handed me the slate, the Army Officer added softly, Look, this is a magic slate.

You can write on it, then erase it like magic. And just as a prayer can wipe away bad fortune and write a better destiny, so can this slate help you dream and rewrite your future.

These words, as Abbi later told me, had touched everyone present.

I, of course, had forgotten that part over the years. I only remembered the slate itself the precious slate.

(And yes, this was the very same slate I mentioned at the beginning of this story the slate that had carried the hopes of a little girl growing up in captivity, holding fast to dreams of freedom.)

After that, the distribution of prizes to the children began. Some received toys, others were given Ludo sets.

Every child seemed delighted with their reward. Semi Appa won first prize a Ludo board, while Nadeem was thrilled to receive a children's cricket set.

Nazia and Rehan were each given a doll and a ball. In fact, every child received a gift, whether they had won a game or not.

The entire camp beamed with joy. Then sweets were handed out to everyone.

On the men's side, the cricket and football players were awarded their prizes.

The captain of the winning team was given a large bundle containing Margo soap, toothpaste, biscuits, and even cigarettes a much-appreciated luxury. Other players received Margo soap and biscuits.

Finally, the helicopter returned to take the guests away, and so, the day of August 15th came to an end an unforgettable day of joy amidst captivity.

Time continued to pass at its own unhurried pace. In the meantime, life inside the camp evolved. Babies were born, and even weddings took place.

Those young men and women who had lost their families began to express their feelings across the dividing wire, and with the blessing of the elders, several of them were married.

These weddings were simple just a nikah ceremony, but for these young souls, it was a new reason to live.

Even Makhan Sahib, who had long resisted the playful teasing of the boys, finally relented.

The elders explained to him gently that the boys only meant to lighten the mood; in truth, everyone knew his daughters needed a mother. If you agree, they said, we can speak to the women. Perhaps Razia would be willing to marry you.

A year had passed since we had first entered the camp. Eventually, Makhan Sahib agreed, and with the camp authorities' permission, his wedding to Razia was arranged.

On the day of the wedding, the langar prepared special food. That night, the boys celebrated with dancing and by beating the empty cooking pots like drums, creating a cheerful ruckus that echoed into the night.

These simple joys were all we prisoners had. When a baby was born, the women gathered to sew little clothes and prepare food.

It felt as if everyone had forgotten they were prisoners, living not in captivity, but in a close-knit village or neighbourhood.

This prison camp had become a community, a life both removed from the world and yet so close to the essence of living.

We rarely knew what happened in the neighbouring camp, hidden beyond layers of barbed wire.

But whenever there was music or celebration on our side, we would see faces peering from the distance, quietly watching.

As for me, I had never once stepped outside the camp. Only the seriously ill or those giving birth were taken beyond the wire and even then, under heavy army guard.

One day, because of me, even Abbi had to leave the camp and go to the hospital.

It happened like this: we children were playing a game something like a version of hide-and-seek where we had to keep changing corners.

I had always been quick on my feet and determined never to lose. That day was no different. Two children guarded the door, two stood by the pillars, and a "thief" waited in the middle to tag anyone who ran.

As I darted toward the door to avoid being caught, the child at the door stuck out his leg playfully. The door was already ajar. In my haste, I crashed straight into the edge of the doorframe. It struck me just above the eye, and blood immediately gushed out like a fountain.

Ammi rushed out, panic flooding her face. Seeing the blood pouring from my head, she began to cry, fearing I might have injured my eye. A commotion erupted in the camp. The doctor hurried over and pressed cotton against the wound to stop the bleeding.

This will need stitches, he said gravely. And a proper examination at the hospital.

Within moments, army personnel arrived. A phone call was made. An army truck soon rolled in, its back covered by a tarpaulin.

By then, the camp doctor had administered first aid. He told Ammi and Abbi, one of you must accompany the child.

The army officer confirmed it. Only one person can go. Which of you will it be?

I will go, Abbi said firmly, placing a reassuring hand on Ammi's shoulder. You stay here with the rest of the children.

The army soldiers clasped a handcuff around Abbi's wrist. I looked at him, wide-eyed. It's necessary, one of them explained gently.

Abbi climbed into the back of the truck, holding me in his lap. Soldiers sat along the edges, silent and watchful, and the tarp was drawn down behind us. I couldn't stop crying.

My head throbbed, and the fear was almost worse than the pain. The soldiers tried to soothe me, speaking softly.

Along the way, they explained to Abbi and me, we're taking you to the army hospital. Don't speak to anyone there. Don't answer any questions. We'll speak on your behalf.

When we arrived, the hospital was crowded. Two soldiers accompanied us inside. This was the Army Family Hospital.

People stared as we passed the man in handcuffs holding a bleeding child. Their eyes seemed to ask, what crime have you committed? Who are you? What have you done?

The pain was unbearable. Blood still trickled down my face.

Twice, Abbi asked a nurse to attend me. The third time, she snapped harshly, Be quiet! God knows what crime you've committed, and now you dare to give orders too?

The Indian army guard, standing silently in the corner, swiftly approached and said sharply, Take the child inside immediately and do your job. No unnecessary talk.

Then, lowering his voice but filled with authority, he added, I'll be reporting you for this. You've done this before.

The nurse's face paled. She quickly took me into the examination room.

Inside, she asked, who are you? Who's that man with you?

Abbi, I whispered.

Where have you come from?

Before I could answer, the soldier entered. Didn't I tell you not to question them?

Just then, the doctor arrived. He gently cleaned the wound above my eye.

You were very lucky, he said. The injury just missed your eye. It's swollen shut now. We'll need to stitch it.

After stitching the wound, the doctor said, she'll need rest. Bring her back in fifteen to twenty days to remove the stitches.

The scar on my eyelid, to this day, is the mark of my time as a prisoner of war.

Once the treatment was complete, we returned to the camp.

On the way back, Abbi quietly asked the army guard, could you lift the curtain just a little? I want to catch a glimpse of Meerut.

The soldier nodded and lifted the tarp slightly. Abbi looked out, his eyes drinking in the view. I peeked out too, catching my first fleeting glimpse of Meerut a city that had become a distant, unreachable dream.

Abbi sighed, almost to himself. One day, he whispered, if life permits and destiny allows, I will walk freely through Meerut again.

As the truck rolled along, carrying us back to what was now our world whether one called it a home or a prison it was all we had.

Fifteen or twenty days later, we returned to the army hospital. The stitches were removed. The scar would remain, but the wound had healed.

Back at the camp, life returned to its old rhythm. Among my siblings, my eldest sister was the most sensible and studious. Throughout our imprisonment, she was either by Ammi and Nani's side or caring for our younger siblings. If not, she could always be found with a book in hand.

But my sister, Semi Appa, always had one persistent complaint, there was never any meat in our meals.

Ammi sometimes managed to buy eggs from the camp canteen and boiled them for the younger children.

But Semi Appa didn't want boiled eggs. She wanted them fried.

In those days, her greatest desire in life seemed to revolve around meat and fried eggs. Simple wishes. Yet, in captivity, even such small luxuries felt out of reach.

Nadeem and Rehan made it a daily ritual to circle around the camp canteen.

The canteen keeper had a habit of pulling little plastic animals from Cibaca toothpaste boxes and handing them to children.

If too many children gathered, he would toss the toys into the air, and whatever child caught them would keep them.

I often teamed up with my two younger brothers in the scramble to grab the prizes.

In those days, Cibaca toothpaste boxes came with small surprises hidden inside tiny gifts meant for children. Over time, Nadeem and Rehan became quite friendly with the canteen uncle.

He took a liking to them and, whenever possible, secretly slipped them the little gifts from inside the toothpaste boxes making sure to hide this from the other children to avoid any quarrels.

Even in captivity, the small joys of childhood found their way into our lives.

The war had left deep scars on Rehan and Nazia. Rehan had been so traumatized that he developed a stutter, unable to fully express himself.

Even today, though he no longer stammers, he keeps his thoughts locked away, never truly sharing what lies in his heart.

For Nazia, the impact was different. Her entire world revolved around two things: the little pillow she clung to at all times and Nani (our grandmother).

During the chaos of war and our frantic escape, it was our grandmother who had held her close, comforting her through every terror-filled night.

Even in the camp, Rehan and Nazia could not be separated from their Nani (grandmother), just as Nadeem could not bear to be apart from Ammi.

The shadows of war and captivity lingered in all of us. They remained buried deep in our subconscious, taking the shape of silent fears and uncertainties that haunted us in quiet, persistent ways.

When our Nani passed away, Nazia struggled to adjust to life without her. She found it nearly impossible to share her feelings or be understood by anyone else.

Those hidden terrors still linger in my siblings' hearts, manifesting as doubts and anxieties they might not even recognize or perhaps refuse to remember.

But I do not forget. I cannot forget. That's why I write so that every memory, every truth, lives on.

Years passed. Another Ramadan came and went, as did Eid and Bakra Eid. Now, once again, Ramadan was approaching but there was still no word of our freedom.

Yes, there had been one small mercy. Eight months into our captivity, those over the age of sixty had been released. Some from our camp had finally left, carrying with them a bittersweet taste of freedom.

Meanwhile, every morning, news crackled through the loudspeakers, bringing updates from the outside world.

We heard whispers that the Simla Agreement was in the making, and with it, the possibility of prisoner releases.

We clung to that hope, living each day on the fragile promise that news of our freedom might come at any moment.

There was much in this prison routine, moments of joy, even the semblance of a community. But there was no freedom.

No freedom to see loved ones. No freedom to return home. No freedom to live as we once had. Only the constant waiting.

People were slowly becoming accustomed to this life. The prison had begun to feel like their homeland, and the small spaces they occupied within it had become their homes.

They marked their territories not with walls but with whatever they had hammering nails into the wooden beams and stretching cords across the space to hang makeshift curtains. Some used old sarees, others stitched together dupattas or even patched cloth. These simple dividers signified that this was a family's space. A silent message that no one else should enter.

Ammi, too, had claimed our small corner. She tied a rope from one end to the other and carefully stitched together sarees to form a curtain.

A frail barrier but one that gave us a sense of privacy, a fragment of dignity.

Who would have thought that a woman from such a grand house would one day live like this humbly dividing her space with fabric, living conditions no servant in her former home had ever endured?

Thus, in that bare barrack room, our family claimed the farthest corner. Within our space stood four charpoys. In the evenings, Ammi often cooked little treats, sometimes custard, sometimes kheer, sometimes a simple egg and potato dish using the lingering warmth of the community kitchen's large, empty stove.

She would send them across the barbed wire to Abbi.

Sometimes, at dusk, my parents stood at either side of the fence and spoke softly. Not about our uncertain future but of old memories, of family left behind.

The women in the camp often argued. Petty quarrels broke out over whose turn it was to bathe, who would wash clothes first, who would use the cooking fires, or which child had struck another.

Yet, I never once saw Ammi argue. If anyone scolded her about the children, she would simply listen in silence and then gently explain things to us.

At night, all of us children gathered around Nani to hear her stories. For my youngest siblings, Rehan and Nazia, their entire world revolved around Nani.

Abbi, when his duties were done, would watch us children at play. Sometimes he joined in football games or sat with us for a round of carrom.

Often, when Abbi played carrom with us, he would be my partner so I could have a chance to win. Nadeem would pair up with Semi Appa. Semi Appa, of course, would cheat by secretly pocketing the queen.

At first, arguments would flare up. But soon, Abbi would pretend to lose, making us laugh. I always protested when he let them win, and Nadeem would cheer proudly at his victory even if it came by Semi Appa's clever cheating.

These were our little joys. Simple, fleeting moments but in that place, they felt like the greatest joys in the world.

A strange and puzzling incident once happened to me in the camp something none of us have ever been able to fully explain, even now.

At the very end of our barrack, just before the row of bathrooms, there was a large open ground. In that ground lay three pits, partly concealed with branches and twigs. No one remembered exactly when or why those pits had been dug, but we were all used to walking past them daily.

One afternoon, I suddenly disappeared. The camp searched everywhere. No trace of me. The soldier in the tower was questioned.

He said, the children were playing here, but then they all scattered and went off.

Maybe she's just wandered into another barrack.

All the children were gathered and asked where I had gone, but nobody knew.

By four o'clock, then five, panic had begun to spread. Abbi, now frantic, went to the army office and requested permission to enter the women's side of the camp.

A few army officers also came and began questioning the children.

One child finally spoke up: Rosy was playing near the pit. After that, we didn't see her.

Everyone rushed toward the pits. Branches and logs were removed from the first pit empty. The second also empty.

Then, as soon as Abbi pulled away the branches from the third pit, he saw me.

I was sitting calmly at the bottom, playing with my doll. Not crying. Not afraid of the darkness.

Rosy Abbi gasped. What are you doing here? How did you fall? What happened?

With perfect calm, I looked up at him and answered, I'm playing with my friend. But when you all came, he ran away.

Abbi and the others exchanged grave, worried glances. The only explanation they could imagine was that perhaps an older boy had lured me there for mischief and fled when the adults arrived.

But deep down, no one was truly sure what had happened that day.

The officer took me by the hand and led me from barrack to barrack. At each stop, he pointed to different boys, asking gently,
Was it this child? Every time, my answer was the same.

No, that's not the boy. He's not the one.

The soldiers wanted to catch whoever it was to scold him, to make sure no harm would come to me again.

But how could they, when there was no boy to be found?

What truly happened that day, none of us ever discovered.

What baffled my parents most and still does to this day was how calmly I had been sitting at the bottom of that deep pit.

It was deep enough that a grown man could stand inside it. A child might fall in, yes, but climbing out alone would have been impossible.

And yet, there I had been. Sitting quietly. Unafraid. Untroubled.

After the incident, someone advised Abbi, don't let the children play near that spot anymore.

I, however, never remembered the event myself.

It was only much later that Abbi recounted the entire story to me and asked that I include it in this memoir.

Then, one day, something happened that would change our family's story yet again.

Ammi had fallen ill. At first, it seemed like one of her usual spells of weakness, but when Abbi took her to the camp doctor, he returned with news that filled his heart with both joy and sorrow.

A new life was on the way. The doctor had confirmed that Ammi was expecting.

It should have been a moment of pure happiness a sign that even in captivity, life continued, that hope refused to be extinguished. But for Abbi, happiness came shadowed by worry.

Yes, the family would grow, but at what cost? What kind of world was this child about to be born into?

We children, wrapped up in our own little world, were oblivious to the gravity of this news.

We only knew that Ammi often felt unwell now.

Without fully understanding why, we had begun turning to our older sister, Semi Appa, and our Nani for every little need. They had become our pillars.

Prison is still prison, no matter how much one tries to make it feel like home.

There was food, yes but just enough to keep us alive.

You could call it sustenance, perhaps, but never nourishment.

Certainly not the kind of food a pregnant woman required to keep herself and her child healthy.

Abbi did all he could to keep Ammi's spirits up. That was the one luxury he could still afford.

But there were other hardships. Abbi couldn't help with the children much, his days were spent working on the men's side of the camp, allowed to cross the wire only for two brief hours each day.

Whenever Ammi needed to see the doctor, Abbi would accompany her to the camp's small clinic.

And when he could, he used our limited camp coupons to buy whatever little necessities he could from the canteen.

Among the women of the camp, there was a beautiful tradition.

Whenever joyful news graced any family, like the promise of a new child, everyone came together to prepare little things for the baby, crafting them from old fabrics.

So, just as the others had done before her, Ammi began to prepare for the arrival of her child.

She carefully cut pieces from the end of her own sari, sewing tiny clothes for the newborn.

Nani, too, took one of her old saris and fashioned it into small blankets.

Some women made simple cloth toys. One crafted tiny bird, hanging them on strings so they could dangle above the baby's sleeping place a handmade version of what the world now calls a *rattle toy*.

In those days, instead of music-playing mobiles, mothers would gently sway such toys in their hands to amuse their infants.

Everyone, in their own way, brought small gifts for the baby and offered Ammi their wisdom and advice.

The women of the camp, despite their hardships, had found a purpose once more. The simple joy of preparing for a new life united them all.

During this time, news finally arrived the prisoners of war were being released, though in small groups.

Though, as we later learned, repatriations had quietly begun as early as December 1972, it wasn't until January 1973 that the news reached us.

A wave of joy swept through the camp. People congratulated each other, laughter and hope returning to faces worn by waiting.

But amid the excitement, uncertainty lingered. No one knew when our turn would come or how we would be sent home.

Each day, the camp radio announced how many prisoners had been freed. We listened intently, holding our breath. Yet, as the numbers grew, so too did our restlessness.

When will it be us? became the unspoken question in every heart.

Despite the joy, a quiet sorrow remained. The Army officers had not yet given us any news, and so we waited still caged, though the door seemed, finally, to be creaking open.

December 3 to 16, 1971. just one week and six days of war had shattered countless homes, leaving deep scars in its wake.

Now, there was at last a glimmer of hope. The promise of returning home seemed within reach.

Yet no one could say for certain whether that hope would bear fruit.

Abbi too had begun to wonder what lay ahead. Where would we go? How would we live if we were released?

And a heavier worry tugged at his heart would the coming child be born here, in captivity, or in freedom?

If the baby was born after our release, how would we manage the hospital costs? Who would help us then? Life moved forward in this state of anxious waiting.

But Nani always tried to calm Abbi's fears. Son, she would say gently, don't let these thoughts trouble you.

God has kept us safe this far. He will see us through what lies ahead. Just keep your faith in Him.

Every soul in the camp was restless now. Everyone waited, their eyes fixed on the horizon.

When would the news of release finally come?

Then, one day, the moment we had all prayed for finally arrived.

The Army officer came into the camp and gathered everyone together.

His voice was calm but carried a weight that stilled the restless crowd.

I ask all of you to listen carefully and remain calm, he began.

The two governments have agreed to release the prisoners. Some have already begun their journey home.

A ripple of excitement swept through the people, but he raised a hand for silence.

It is not possible to release everyone at once. You will all leave in different groups. This process could take months or even a year.

A hushed murmur spread among the camp. Faces once dull with despair now showed a fragile hope.

You too, the officer continued, will leave from this camp. Please be patient. Groups will be formed soon.

At this, the crowd could no longer contain themselves. Cries rose from every corner Please, put us in the first list! Let us go first.

But Singh Sahib, standing beside the officer, called out firmly, Everyone, be quiet.

There's no need for shouting. All of you will return home every single one of you.

His words washed over the crowd like a balm. People began to weep softly not from sorrow, but from the relief of hope finally becoming real.

Go now, Singh Sahib added gently. Go and prepare to leave.

The news had arrived at the very beginning of the year. The moment it spread through the camp, people fell to the ground in prostration, tears of gratitude spilling onto the dusty earth.

Everyone began to pray desperately, let our names be in the first list.

Preparations began immediately as if they would be leaving the very next day.

The joy was so overwhelming it was almost too much for many to bear.

That night, the young men beat the cooking cauldrons like drums and danced in the open yard until the early hours, celebrating not just freedom, but the return of hope.

The next evening, as the women gathered on the usual tarp spread out across the ground, they turned to Ammi.

Your unborn child is blessed, they said. This child is the messenger of good news for all of us.

The one soul destined to enter this world bearing the promise that our days of hardship are finally ending, and that freedom has come.

Though happiness filled the air, so did sorrow. Ahead lay the journey but no clear destination.

What they had built with their hard work in East Pakistan had been left behind in Bangladesh.

The few family members who survived were scattered some parents, some siblings still in India.

Others had relatives in Pakistan, but no one knew what kind of welcome awaited them there.

Where would they settle? How would they earn a living? Their documents had been left behind in the chaos of war.

Now, as they stood at the threshold between captivity and freedom, there was no support but God's mercy. Only He knew what lay ahead.

The following month, a much-awaited list arrived at our camp, naming the families scheduled to leave in the next group.

The chosen families; fifteen or twenty in total were told to prepare for departure. Our names were not among them.

More prisoners were being released than could be sent at once, so they were being gathered from multiple camps and transported in batches.

The delays were frustrating, but we knew safety protocols and the terms of the Shimla Agreement dictated the pace.

Those selected for release were overjoyed. The rest of us watched them with bittersweet longing, our own hopes clinging to the promise of a future departure.

As more families left, the remaining prisoners were consolidated into the vacant barracks.

The camp itself seemed to grow quieter and emptier, its once bustling lanes losing their familiar vibrancy.

Two groups had already departed from our camp.

Then, amidst this dwindling crowd, our family received its own momentous news.

The time had come; Ammi had to be taken to the army hospital.

She gathered the few things she had a small cloth blanket fashioned from her old sari, and a larger sheet stitched together from my grandmother's sari. Labor pains gripped her fiercely.

By the mercy of God, after a long struggle, a new life arrived. A baby girl.

Tears slipped silently down Abbi's face. He whispered words that have echoed in my heart ever since.

There is no doubt when God sends a daughter into the world, He sends her with this decree, Go, your father's livelihood is My responsibility.

And indeed, my little sister had entered this world bearing the message of freedom.

Ammi, though weary and aching, longed to buy something special for her newborn a bottle, perhaps, or a new outfit.

But coupons, the only currency allowed in camp, were worthless in the outside world. Still, she was determined.

Without hesitation, she slipped the gold ring from her finger and offered it to the nurse.

Please, she said softly, sell this and buy my daughter a glass feeding bottle and a couple of new outfits.

The nurse took the ring and returned the next day with the items. Your ring fetched only 14 rupees, she explained. I added the rest from my own pocket. Consider it a gift.

Ammi asked no questions. She was simply grateful that, even amidst captivity, her child had something new something born not of hardship, but of hope.

Three days later, Ammi was discharged from the hospital.

Abbi, meanwhile, had a strong sense that the army officer in charge had deliberately pushed our names further down the release list.

Perhaps he wanted to ensure Ammi delivered safely before our departure.

After all, she was the only woman in the camp still awaiting childbirth.

When mother returned from the hospital with the newborn, the first concern was what name should they give the baby?

Of course, every child must be named but, in this case, there was added urgency. The child's name had to be entered into the release registry.

Immediately, the women of the camp gathered for a special meeting.

This little girl, born amidst captivity and soldiers, had become precious to everyone.

First, there was a small celebration. Those families who had survived the long ordeal brought humble gifts for the baby especially the beloved little cloth bird, lovingly hand-sewn as a rattle.

Then came the important task, choosing a name. Grandmother was the first to suggest something.

I shall call her Fauji, she declared fondly, because she was born surrounded by soldiers.

The women smiled and agreed that while Fauji could be her nickname, the child also needed a proper name something graceful and meaningful.

One woman suggested, why don't we name her Fouzia? It sounds like Fauji, and it also means 'victorious.

Everyone nodded in agreement. And so, it was decided the child's formal name would be Fouzia, but to her grandmother and many others, she would always be their little Fauji.

Fouzia was only a few months old when the long-awaited list finally arrived the names of the next group of prisoners who would be released and repatriated.

Our family was on the list. The news spread through the camp like wildfire.

The memories of yesterday, of the long, painful journey, of loss and survival, came rushing back to my parents.

Overcome with gratitude and disbelief, they fell to their knees in sajdah, offering their heartfelt prayers of thanks.

It was true. After everything, we were finally going home. We were going to be free.

****

THE JOURNEY TO FREEDOM

Since Abbi had heard the news that we were finally leaving, a deep restlessness had overtaken him.

What would become of us now? What awaited us in West Pakistan?

His parents were still here, his family home, lands, and property were all here too. And the cruel twist of fate was that despite owning a home, we could not return to it nor could we meet his parents, brothers, or sisters again.

Where would we go? No one knew where they would even drop us off.

We had no money, no jobs waiting for us, and not even the proper documents that might help us find work. There would be no shelter either.

Days passed in this torment of uncertainty. Ammi began gathering our meager belongings how would we carry it all?

We had just one small, black metal trunk. The rest of our possessions included a few plates, some clothes, and whatever else could be bundled into a cloth sack.

And then there was the smallest member of our family a baby girl who had only recently entered this world.

Nazia clung fiercely to her little pillow. That pillow was her protector, her toy, her everything.

Nani made it very clear, no matter what else stayed behind, that pillow would go with us. She would not let anyone touch it.

Often, Nani would curse the day she had travelled from India to East Pakistan (Bangladesh) to visit her daughter.

She'd say, if only I hadn't stayed back out of love for my daughter and grandchildren, at least then I could have provided you all with everything you needed. You would have had a home and some stability.

Though Nani's heart did not want to leave India behind, she had no choice now. She had to go because Ammi was her only daughter.

As the days of our departure drew nearer, an unexpected sorrow began to creep into our hearts.

Why, we wondered, did the sight of this camp and its barracks once symbols of our captivity now stir a deep sadness within us?

Memories of the time we had spent here, through hardship and fleeting joys alike, came rushing back.

By now, only a few families remained in the barracks. At night, fear gripped us even more than before; walking alone to the bathroom became a daunting task.

Even during the day, an eerie stillness hung over the camp. Everyone had moved into just two remaining barracks, silently counting the days until departure.

We didn't know if the people in the neighbouring camp had already left or were still waiting for their turn.

Finally, by the grace of God our day to leave arrived.

The day before we were to depart, the army officer came to address us.

Tomorrow, he announced, you will begin your journey. First, there will be a personal check and then your belongings will be inspected.

Please do not carry anything that might cause trouble during the checking process.

Any valuables or documents that were taken from you at the time of your arrival will be returned to you.

Do not take anything from the camp that does not belong to you.

He paused for a moment, as if choosing his next words carefully.

Whether life brings us together again or not is in God's hands. But know this; this chapter of life, this time spent together, will remain in my memory as much as in yours.

This time has been not just a story, but a living, breathing memory for all of us.

Thank you for the way you cooperated with us during this long and difficult period.

A hush fell over the group.

Later, the officer added, please come to the office to collect your belongings.

Abbi stepped forward and spoke to the army officer with quiet dignity.

Sir, we do not know if we will ever meet again, he began. But after coming here, we have realized one thing your own people remain your own, no matter what.

The time we have spent in this camp has proven to us that humanity, compassion, and brotherhood still exist in this world.

We are deeply grateful for the kindness you have shown us and the way you tried so hard to make sure we never felt like prisoners.

The army officer then called me over. His expression had softened, and his eyes glistened with unshed tears.

Look, my child, he said, today my promise has been fulfilled. The birds I spoke of are finally going free.

(Abbi shared these words with me years later, when we were writing down this story together.)

As the officer spoke, tears filled not only his eyes but also those of every person gathered their families who had endured months of uncertainty and sorrow together.

These tears were not just of sadness but of shared understanding.

They stood as proof that love needs no language. It doesn't matter who you are, where you come from, or what side of a conflict you may find yourself on.

When you speak the language of humanity, divisions like race, religion, enmity, even the line between jailer and prisoner they all disappear.

What remains is humanity. What remains is love.

Afterward, a group photograph was taken. First, one of all the families preparing to leave. Then, at the officer's request, another photograph was taken just of our family.

Back then, the camera was the kind where the photo would develop and print out immediately.

The officer showed us the picture.

Abbi asked politely, could we have another taken, and perhaps a copy for ourselves? It would be a keepsake for us.

The officer smiled sadly. Mr. Shamim, he replied, I wish I could. But if you carry this photograph across the border, it could cause you trouble during the inspections.

Let this picture remain in our records. It will always be a reminder for both of us.

Then, with a brief, silent nod, the officer turned and left.

One by one, everyone went to the office to reclaim whatever belongings they had entrusted to the authorities.

Ammi received back the few pieces of jewellery she had left with them. As for Abbi he had no official papers to collect.

He gathered what little they had, said his goodbyes, and returned to the barracks with a heavy heart.

A thousand thoughts weighed on his mind. I have no educational certificates; once we are free, what work will I do? How will I provide?

The small amount of jewellery they retrieved would perhaps help them get by for a short while. After that, it would be only God's mercy guiding their path.

Abbi, Ammi and Nani spent the evening making sure everything was ready the humble bundle of belongings, the small black trunk, the children's few clothes and bedding.

The family gathered what little they owned and waited.

Now, there was only one thing left, the official word on what time they would leave in the morning. The long-awaited journey to freedom was finally at the doorstep.

That night, word finally arrived: they would depart at dawn.

Everyone was told to sleep early. But sleep is a stranger on the eve of freedom.

At 4 A.M., the family stirred from restless slumber. Outside, soldiers were already bustling about, making final preparations. Large army trucks rolled in and lined up.

The same groups that had arrived together in captivity would now return together in liberty or at least, toward the uncertain promise of it.

Families hurried to ready themselves. The children were dressed in their cleanest, simplest clothes.

A modest breakfast was shared in quiet anticipation. Then, everyone gathered and lined up for the final headcount.

Afterward, as was tradition among the prisoners, people embraced one another and asked forgiveness.

If I have ever wronged you or caused you pain forgive me.

Even Tiwari ji and Pandit ji, the guards who had once loomed like watchful sentinels but had long since become familiar, even beloved figures stood nearby.

Father embraced them both. Everyone was crying.

Tiwari ji and Pandit ji looked toward me and my brother Nadeem, shaking their heads with fond exasperation. Always causing mischief, you two, they scolded gently.

Then, turning to Semi Appa, they added, and you, your problems are over now.

You'll get to cook your eggs however you like. And there will be meat every day. You'll be living in luxury.

Their teasing was betrayed by tears streaming down their faces. It felt not like leaving a prison but like parting from family.

A farewell to a place that had, against all odds, become home.

A farewell to people with whom they had shared sorrow, resilience, and the faint, fragile joys that bloom even in captivity. They all understood.

This was a journey from which no one would return not to this place, not to this chapter of life.

Even those who had departed before had felt the same ache.

Then began the final inspection. One by one, all family's belongings were checked.

As each inspection was completed, families were directed to stand near the camp gate within the barbed wire enclosure that had once imprisoned them, and now became the passageway to freedom.

Truck after truck was driven inside and lined up across the central ground. The massive vehicles waited, their open backs ready to carry lives uprooted by war.

A soldier stepped forward, a list in hand. As names are called, he announced, those families will board the trucks. Young men, help the elderly and children climb aboard.

The names began echoing across the grounds. As each family approached, representatives from the Red Cross handed out a box and a cloth bag filled with food supplies for adults and children alike.

Ammi had already prepared a bottle of milk for little Fouzia, the daughter born behind barbed wires, the child of captivity and of hope. But still, she was given another tin of powdered milk. The gesture brought back a flood of memories.

Ammi's eyes clouded as she remembered those desperate days of flight and fear, when Rehan and Nazia, as toddlers, had drunk nothing but "maarh" rice water because no milk could be found. Nani (grandmother) had poured the warm, starchy liquid into bottles and fed it to the crying children, whispering prayers they might survive until better days.

And now, standing at the threshold of freedom, Ammi clutched her new supplies with silent gratitude.

We were not told exactly where we were going or how we would get there. All we knew the only thing that mattered was that we were finally going to Pakistan.

Instructions were clear. When the trucks stop, no one is to pull back the curtains.

Once all families had boarded, the soldiers called out names one final time to ensure no one was left behind. Then, slowly, the convoy rumbled forward.

As the trucks rolled out of the camp, our hearts pounded in unison. After twenty-two long months as prisoners of war, we were finally on the road to freedom.

Through the small gaps in the curtain, we watched the camp the only home many of us had known for nearly two years grow smaller and smaller behind us.

Father was happy, yes. But a quiet sorrow also flickered in his eyes.

Even if it was behind barbed wire, he thought, my parents were still in this land.

There had always been hope. Maybe one day, permission would come to see Amma and Abba, to embrace them again.

But now, freedom was pulling us far, far away. So far that the road back would not be just difficult. It would be almost impossible.

As the truck's maneuverer onto the main roads, the soldiers pulled down the heavy canvas curtains surrounding us.

Abbi guessed it was for our safety, to shield us from curious eyes as we passed through towns or settlements.

The truck rumbled on not too fast, not too slow. But Abbi noticed something else. They were deliberately avoiding crowded areas.

After some time, the convoy halted in a desolate stretch of land. A soldier called out, if anyone, young or old, needs to use the washroom, now is the time.

The curtain was lifted briefly. Around us stretched only barren fields. No houses. No people. It felt as though they were waiting for something or someone.

An hour passed. The trucks moved again. Curtains down.

We didn't know how many hours had rolled by. It was all a blur of jolting wheels, hushed whispers, and the rocking rhythm of the road beneath us.

By evening, we arrived at the outskirts of a railway station a remote, uninhabited area. There, the soldiers guided us off the trucks and toward a waiting train.

The train's windows were shuttered. Other families from different camps were boarding into separate compartments.

Beyond the tracks, there was nothing. Just the vast emptiness of land stretching into the horizon.

We climbed aboard. Everyone washed their faces, hands trying to freshen up after the long, hot journey. Those who had saved food unpacked it, sharing what they could.

The children exhausted, ate quickly and soon fell asleep.

Not long after, the train groaned to life, inching forward at a slow, cautious pace. In every carriage, four or five soldiers stood guard.

The train never gathered much speed. When it paused, it was always at remote outer signals far from any towns or stations.

Sometime deep into the night, lulled by the gentle swaying, we all finally drifted into sleep.

It must have been around four or five in the morning when we were awakened.

The soldiers moved briskly through the train, calling out for everyone to gather their belongings and disembark quickly.

Ammi gently woke us children, helping us wash our faces and hands. She gathered our few possessions mostly the small trunk and the bundles of clothes wrapped in cloth. We're ready, she told Abbi.

One by one, we climbed down from the train into the crisp early morning air. Waiting outside were more army trucks.

We were told though the memory has blurred with time that we had arrived at Amritsar railway station, or perhaps somewhere nearby.

Once again, a roll call was conducted. Every name from the list was called. Families were accounted for. Then, slowly, we boarded the trucks.

This time, however, the canvas curtains were not drawn down. The open road stretched before us.

We could see the greenery of the countryside, the trees swaying gently in the morning breeze.

For the first time in many months, we travelled without the feeling of being hidden from the world.

There was a strange, quiet excitement among us. And then, as the trucks rolled forward, we approached a place we had only heard of in stories and whispered dreams the historic border known as Wagah.

This was no ordinary road. It was the same path where, in the aftermath of the great Partition of 1947, thousands had once crossed hopeful, fearful, determined.

That day, history was repeating itself.

In 1947, Brigadier (later Major General) Mahinder Chopra and Brigadier Nazir Ahmad had first established the Wagah crossing.

It had become a symbol of parting and of reunions, of endings and beginnings.

Now, once again, people were crossing. Not migrants. Not refugees.

But prisoners of war or, as we had come to see ourselves, survivors of a time that had changed everything.

The Wagah border, located about 32 kilometers from Amritsar in Punjab, stands as the crossing point between Amritsar (India) and Lahore (Pakistan).

Our convoy of trucks came to a stop on the Indian side of the border. We were asked to disembark.

All around us, the scene was carefully organized. Soldiers and members of the Red Cross stood at their stations.

Long rows of tables had been set up along the road, their surfaces covered with drinks, dry snacks like biscuits and cakes, samosas, and various fruit juices.

At the first three tables sat officials from both the Indian Army and the Red Cross.

An officer stepped forward and gave instructions.

Please form a line with your families. Answer whatever questions are asked.

You may also take any food or drinks you need from the tables as you proceed.

It was late morning perhaps around 11 or noon. The exact time and date have blurred in my memory, but I recall the weight of the moment pressing heavily on all of us.

Slowly, steadily, our group began to move forward.

When our turn came, an army officer asked Abbi for his name and my grandfather's name.

Then he requested the names of every family member and conducted a headcount.

Once everything was noted, he handed Abbi a folded paper.

Keep this with you, he instructed. You'll need to show it further ahead.

With that, we were waved forward, inching closer to the line where two nations met and where our long captivity was finally nearing its end.

As we moved forward, the atmosphere became unexpectedly festive.

Colourful **balloons** were tied along the way, and they were being handed out to the children.

We eagerly took ours, the simple joy momentarily distracting us from the long road ahead.

But amidst the cheer, there was a frantic energy too. The volunteers placing food and snacks on the tables were struggling to keep up.

Each time they unpacked a box and laid out the items, the tables were cleared within moments.

Adults and children alike gathered the biscuits, cakes, and samosas hungrily as if afraid there would be nothing to eat beyond this place.

Perhaps it was the long years of deprivation, or perhaps it was simply the thrill of abundance after so much scarcity.

We children clutched whatever treats we could gather. The line stretched long and moved slowly.

We had not yet reached the Indian border gate itself. Chairs were placed here and there along the way for the elderly and mothers with small children to rest.

Light music played in the background its sweetness mingling with the bittersweet mood.

Those who paused to rest were urged on by their family members. Get up quickly! If we don't cross in time, the gates might close.

Abbi thought, not for the first time, of the great migration of 1947. Then, thousands had made this same journey, leaving behind their homes, sacrificing their lives in the wake of partition to reach their newly formed homelands.

Now, 24 years later, here we were walking the same path. But this was a different kind of journey.

Not the birth of a nation, but the painful aftermath of a nation torn apart.

That had been the journey to national freedom. This was our personal journey to freedom a freedom born of displacement, captivity, and heartbreaking loss. Step by step, we reached the Indian gate.

Now, just a short distance away stood the gate that led into Pakistan.

Our footsteps slowed as the weight of the moment sank in.

The distance between the two gates felt immeasurably long and unbearably heavy.

Finally, we stood before the gate. The moment of crossing had come. Abbi paused and looked back.

In that single glance, he seemed to take in everything we were leaving behind

His mother and father. His brothers and sisters. His land. His childhood. His youth.

Everything was now out of reach including his educational degrees, left behind in East Pakistan, now known as Bangladesh, and ahead? Only uncertainty. But also, at last freedom.

At the gate, a surprising scene awaited us. Some film stars had gathered, smiling warmly as they welcomed us. A few political leaders were also present. The welcome was grand and heartfelt.

Crowds lined both sides of the path. On one side stood celebrities from the film world. On the other, Red Cross officials and political figures greeted us, gently placing garlands of flowers around our necks.

It was a moment of celebration but for many of us, it was a bittersweet victory.

After moving a little further, we reached another series of tables. This time, Pakistani Army officials and Red Cross staff were seated there.

They asked Abbi for his name, my grandfather's name, and family details just as the Indian officials had. The slip of paper we had received at the Indian border was collected and replaced with a new slip, identifying us as official arrivals in Pakistan.

Keep this slip carefully, they told us. It is your proof of entry into Pakistan.

Again, there were long rows of tables lined with food. We ate as we moved forward, and just like before many people filled their bags with as much food as they could carry.

After years of scarcity, no one wanted to leave anything behind.

But it was not just hunger that drove them. It was the instinct of people who had been refugees and prisoners those who knew that in an uncertain tomorrow, even a handful of biscuits could mean survival.

From there, we were taken to what they called a refugee camp or rather, a temporary shelter.

To us, it looked just like another army camp, but nobody really knew where we were exactly, nor did anyone seem to care.

Many people were already there, families who had arrived before us. Others had come and gone, moving on to whatever lay ahead.

We were told, wash up, get settled, and then proceed to the dining area where food is being served.

Ammi and Nani sat with the younger children while Abbi, along with Nadeem and Rehan, went to freshen up.

He washed and changed the boys' clothes, then returned to watch over the family and guard our belongings.

That modest bundle of possessions hardly more than a few clothes and plates was now all we owned. But to us, it felt like a treasure chest.

Then it was our turn. Nani, Ammi, Semi Appa, Nazia, and then headed toward the large hall where people were gathering.

Families who had already eaten were leaving, making room for others.

The meal was biryani, raita, and salad. But no one cared much for raita or salad. All they wanted was the biryani and especially the qorma.

Semi Appa looked like it was Eid for her. The trays of biryani and qorma would arrive, and within moments, they would vanish into eager hands.

The servers, growing frustrated, kept pleading, please be patient! Take it easy there's enough for everyone.

But who could listen? After years of hunger and captivity, biryani and freedom had arrived together.

After finishing our meal, we all gathered together and sat in a quiet corner.

Abbi was visibly worried. Yes, we've gained our freedom, but where will I take this large family? Where will we live? How will I earn? What work can I do? the thoughts weighed heavily on his mind.

Nani gently consoled him, Son, always keep faith in God. He has never let us starve nor left us without shelter. He will be our Helper still.

Abbi nodded, yes, Amma. You are my only mother now. Pray that this son of yours can successfully carry the burden of this life's journey with all of you by my side.

Just then, a voice echoed from the loudspeaker.

If anyone in this group has come from East Pakistan (Bangladesh) and was employed by a semi-government or government department, please proceed to the office counters.

Check the lists and provide your details at the designated tables.

Since Pakistan International Airlines (P.I.A) was considered a semi-government organization, this announcement directly concerned Abbi.

Abbi turned to Ammi and said quietly, I should at least go and check. Maybe my name is there. But I have no documents. How will I prove anything?

Ammi gently encouraged him, Take God's name and just go. First, meet them and see.

With a deep breath and a silent prayer, Abbi gathered his courage and stepped outside. He found his way to the P.I.A counter, uncertainty weighing on every step.

When he reached, he said hesitantly, I was also an employee of P.I.A, working in the Works Department. His heart pounded. What if they asked for documents?

Unbeknownst to him, the government offices had formed special committees, called Employee War Prisoner Displaced Persons Rehabilitation Committees.

Representatives from these committees were seated at the counters, recording the returnees' details.

An officer looked up and asked, Your name?

Shamim Ahmed Khan; Abbi replied.

Your father's name?

Abbi gave that too.

Then the officer asked, do you remember your employee number?

No, Abbi admitted. But I do remember the department.

The officer nodded and said, Alright. Check the department list for your name.

Abbi silently recited a prayer and went to check. After a few tense moments, his name appeared on the list.

Relief flooded through him. He hurried back to the officer.

Yes, sir. My name and full details are listed under this number.

The officer opened a large register and verified the entry. Then he asked, did you receive any papers when you arrived?

Yes! Abbi replied quickly.

Please hand that over, the officer requested.

Abbi pulled out the small slip he had been given at the Pakistan border the only document in his possession and handed it to the officer.

Then he said nervously, Brother, I have no educational documents or certificates. If you ask for those, I won't be able to provide them.

He held his breath, fearing this might end his last hope.

The officer smiled and replied, No need. When you first joined, all employee documents were sent to the Karachi head office. Your file is there.

He pointed to the register. Now, just sign your name next to your entry.

Abbi signed; his hands slightly trembling.

Where do you want to go? the officer asked.

Karachi, Abbi replied without hesitation.

Very well, the officer said, noting. He writes "Karachi" beside the signature.

He then handed Abbi an envelope. This contains your travel expenses.

You can either stay here for the day or take your family to an old Lahore hotel for the night.

Tomorrow morning, go to the P.I.A. office, get your employment card, complete the paperwork, and arrange your tickets. The office staff will guide you through the process.

Abbi could hardly believe what he was hearing. From having nothing, suddenly, God had opened a path forward.

He didn't even know how much money was in the envelope joy clouded all else. His legs felt unsteady, as though the earth itself was shifting under him.

Brother, can you tell me the address of a hotel? Abbi asked, realizing he had no idea where to go in Lahore.

The officer smiled again, handed him his own card and the card of a nearby hotel. Keep these.

When you reach the hotel, give my card to whoever's at the counter and tell them I sent you. If they have any questions, they can call me directly.

He paused and added, when you're ready to leave, come back. I'll arrange a horse carriage (buggy) to take you, and I'll explain the route.

I'm also giving you the P.I.A. office address and the contact person there. The hotel staff will help with directions.

At that moment, the officer felt to Abbi like an angel sent by God.

Abbi hurried back to where Nani and Ammi were waiting, a wide smile lighting his face.

Amma, your prayers worked! And Najma, he said, turning to Ammi, Your P.I.A. has followed us here, ready to give this unemployed man a job once again.

Upon hearing this, Nani softly said, my son, whatever God does, He does for our good, though it may not seem so at the time.

We do not understand, but He knows what lies ahead. Think about it God knew the trials that were coming.

Your accident in Dhaka, the closing of your business, your joining P.I.A. none of it was mere coincidence. God was preparing us for this very day.

Her words struck deep into Abbi's heart. Both he and Ammi began to weep quietly, overwhelmed by the realization that their hardships had all been part of a divine plan.

At once, they turned to offer a prayer of gratitude, prostrating before God.

Indeed, Abbi whispered, there is no better Planner than Him (GOD)

After offering the Asr prayer, Abbi and Ammi gathered their belongings. Then Abbi went out to arrange for a Tonga (horse carriage).

He found the officer again and said, brother, can you please arrange a Tonga to the hotel? We'll leave today itself.

The officer smiled warmly, arranged the Tonga, and even explained the route to the driver.

Soon Abbi, Ammi, Nani and all us children climbed aboard. For us kids, everything seemed new and wonderful.

Even the simple Tonga ride felt like a grand adventure. As the Tonga trotted along the streets of Lahore, we eagerly took in every sight the bustling bazaars, the narrow lanes, the old buildings.

It reminded Abbi, Ammi and Nani of the alleys of Old Delhi.

Eventually, the Tonga pulled up in front of the hotel.

Abbi helped everyone down from the Tonga, and we all entered the hotel.

At the entrance, a waiter stopped Abbi and asked whom he wanted to meet.

He seemed to be studying our appearance, trying to assess our background.

Abbi replied calmly, I would like to see the manager, and handed over the card given by the officer.

The waiter took the card to the reception. Shortly after, an attendant went to inform the manager.

The manager himself came out and greeted them warmly, saying,

Yes, we've been expecting P.I.A. families here. There's no need for introductions. How many rooms will you need?

Abbi replied, we'll need two rooms.

The manager arranged one double-bed room and one triple-bed room on the first floor, across from each other.

If you'd like, he added kindly, you can have meals served in your rooms. Just tell one of the boys, no need for the women and children to come downstairs.

Abbi took everyone upstairs. The hotel was nice. The rooms were clean and spacious.

Abbi, Ammi, and the baby, Fouzia, settled into one room, while Nani and all the other children stayed in the other.

Nadeem, Rehan, and Nazia were beside themselves with excitement.

They ran around the room touching everything the beds, the sofa, the table and asking about each object. What's this, Abbi? Rehan asked, pointing at the sofa.

Abbi smiled broadly and replied, that's called a sofa.

Rehan tried to repeat it, but ended up calling it "Phoopa." He then climbed onto it, bouncing with joy.

Everyone laughed, cherishing the innocence and happiness of the moment.

That night, when the waiter brought dinner, he looked quite confused. The Same Food we order thrice.

After dinner, the children were put to bed in Nani's room. Abbi returned to his room where Ammi was waiting.

Tomorrow I'll go to the office and see what they say, Abbi told Ammi.

Oh, and let's finally open that envelope and see how much money is inside.

Ammi carefully opened the envelope. Inside was 48,000 rupees.

Abbi had already withdrawn 2,000 rupees from the camp before they left that had been part of his salary and some bonuses paid by the office. He took out another 3,000 rupees and handed it to Ammi.

Keep this safe, he said. We don't know how many days we'll need to stay in the hotel.

For now, God has provided us with shelter and food. As for tomorrow, He is the best of planners.

The next morning, Abbi spoke to the hotel manager before leaving. My wife and children are in the room. I'm heading to the office.

Please keep an eye on them and check if they need anything. I'll settle the bill when I return.

The manager reassured him, don't worry at all. Go ahead.

Abbi asked everyone to stay together in one room, then left the hotel and took a Tonga to the P.I.A. office.

At the office, there was quite a bit of paperwork and several desks to visit. Abbi had to fill out forms, answer questions, and present the slip he had received earlier at the Lahore camp. After the necessary formalities, his new employee card was issued. It read:

Employee - Prisoner of War Rehabilitation Program.

Then an officer asked him, Will you be staying in Lahore or Karachi?

Karachi, Abbi replied confidently.

The officer nodded and asked, when would you like to travel?

In two days, Abbi responded. I'd like to show the children around Lahore and do a little Eid shopping. After all, when we were freed, Ramadan was already underway.

The officer agreed. Fine. Tomorrow morning, go to our airline office and collect your tickets.

He provided the address and added, once you arrive in Karachi, report to the Karachi office two days later so you can officially resume your duties.

Hearing this, it felt as though Abbi's very steps wavered with happiness, as if life itself had surged back into his veins.

Even now, he couldn't fully believe that after such a long and harrowing journey not only were they free, but God had also granted them freedom with sustenance.

They had needed no charity, nor asked anyone for help. Truly, God had been their greatest helper.

Abbi returned to the hotel. Half the day had slipped away with the paperwork at the office, and Ramadan was still underway.

Though none of us were fasting that day, Abbi told the waiter,

We'd like a good Iftar prepared for us this evening.

After eating our Iftar, we all went out to explore the area around the hotel. Abbi bought small toys for us.

We were thrilled, gazing at everything with wide-eyed wonder. Yet none of us ran off or threw tantrums we clung tightly to our parents.

The fear from our captivity still lingered quietly inside us.

The next day, Abbi took us on a Tonga ride around Lahore. The hotel manager had been exceptionally helpful.

In the evening, after settling us children back at the hotel, Abbi and Ammi went out together.

They first visited the airline office and collected our plane tickets. Then they headed to the market and bought Eid clothes for everyone, as well as some new everyday clothes.

Since our flight was scheduled for 3 A.M., they hurried through the shopping.

They also bought a couple of suitcases after all we were about to experience our first ever air travel.

Our belongings were humble: a few bundles of clothes, a small black trunk and, of course, Nazia's cherished pillow. That pillow had survived every journey, every trial.

Abbi turned to Ammi and said, when we reach Karachi, we'll only stay with relatives for as long as it takes to find a place of our own.

Start making a list of household items we'll need. Slowly, we'll gather everything.

Ammi smiled, at least we won't need to buy kitchenware. When you brought us back from West Pakistan to East Pakistan, I hadn't sold the utensils.

I left them with my sister-in-law, packed away in two burlap sacks.

Abbi chuckled softly, even that, I believe, was part of God's greater plan.

We had our dinner by 9 P.M and lay down to sleep early, we had to be at the airport by 1:30 A.M.

That evening, Abbi had already sent telegrams to Luqman Mamoo (Ammi's cousin) and Ashfaq Mamoo (her paternal cousin), informing them that we would arrive the next night.

However, he had forgotten to mention how we were arriving by train or by air.

No one imagined we would actually be arriving by plane.

So, Luqman Mamoo went to the railway station to receive us. Ashfaq Mamoo's address was fresh in Abbi's memory because his house was right opposite Amber Cinema. (He was the same uncle who had once lived with us in Bangladesh but had moved to Karachi just before the fall of Dhaka.)

I still remember it was the 27th night of Ramadan, Shab-e-Qadr, a sacred and blessed night.

At 1:30 A.M., we arrived at the airport and, after clearing all formalities, we proceeded toward our flight.

We children were awestruck, our sense of wonder unending.

This time, when we journeyed, we were dressed in new clothes, and our luggage included two suitcases and the small black trunk that had accompanied us through all the trials of captivity.

Ammi held a beautiful handbag and a lovely plastic basket in which she carried Fouzia's milk bottles and snacks for the children.

That little detail alone spoke volumes; we were free now. And this was the beginning of our journey in freedom.

Once seated on the plane, as it prepared for take-off, Abbi's thoughts were deep and heavy:

This new land the one we are about to call home; how will it welcome us? Will it be kind?

The airplane surged down the runway and soared into the skies. A new chapter of our lives had begun.

For Abbi and Ammi, this journey toward freedom had been long and wearying. Yet, in that moment, a new dawn broke not just for them, but for all of us.

****

CONCLUSION

At the time of their release from captivity, Abbi was 33 years old, and Ammi was 27.

After arriving in Karachi, PIA not only reinstated Abbi's job but also provided him with two and a half years of back pay and bonuses, which helped us secure our own home.

The government arranged for the children of all returning prisoners of war to be admitted to school's midyear. We were enrolled in one of Karachi's finest schools by God's grace.

Abbi had restarted his career in Dhaka, earning 700 rupees, and in Karachi, he resumed with a salary of 1,500 rupees.

It had always been his dream that if he ever visited India again, he would return to the Meerut Army camp where he had once been held. Though he travelled to India three times, fate never allowed him to set foot in Meerut again.

Abbi was never able to meet his mother (my grandmother), Maimoona Khatoon, after captivity. However, in 1977, he, along with Ammi (Najma Khatoon) and my siblings Rehan, Nazia, and Fouzia travelled to *Birnaawa*, our ancestral home.

There, they reunited with family and old acquaintances, including Abbi's mute aunt (whom he had once played with as a child), his father, Dr. Shams-uz-Zaman Khan, and his brother, Naseem Khan, my uncle.

Later, my parents travelled to Patna, to Ammi's ancestral home in Sabzi Bagh, Ismail Manzil. There, they reconnected with her uncle, Dr. Idrees Khan, and other family members.

Ammi entered the very room where she had been born and lived with my grandmother (Nani), Anisa Khatoon.

Nani never returned to India. She carried the sorrow of being unable to revisit her homeland until her passing in 1988.

In 1992, Abbi, Ammi and my sister Anny (Qurratul Ain), who had been born in Karachi, came to India once more, this time to visit me and my daughter, Mahin.

I got married in July 1990, and the year before, my brother Rehan and I had attended a family wedding at Ismail Manzil. That was the first time we both visited India after our release.

Abbi made a final visit to India in 1999, accompanied by Ammi, sisters Fouzia and Nazia, and met my sons Yusuf and Ismail. But despite the visits, a journey to Meerut never materialized.

My brother Nadeem, whose wedding was celebrated in India, visited three times. Yet, my eldest sister, Samina, never managed to visit India. Time and circumstances never allowed

her the opportunity, though she still hopes to one day explore the land of her roots.

Until his last breath, Abbi longed to spend his final days in India. But life never granted that wish.

During the political unrest in Karachi, when the Muhajir Qaumi Movement rose to prominence, I saw Abbi was afraid for the first time.

He was deeply concerned for the safety of his sons. Fear drove him to tell us to always keep important documents and valuables packed in a bag, ready at all times, lest circumstances force us to flee again.

The last six years of his life were spent bedridden. It was during this time, in 2012, that he urged me to write this book.

We often reminisced about the Magic Slate, and he would recount stories from the past.

Though he wished for me to complete this narrative during his lifetime, neither time nor his health permitted it. On January 13, 2013, he departed this world, never witnessing his life story in print.

At Ammi's insistence, and with her help, I finally gathered the courage to fulfil Abbi's last wish to bring to light his life story and the journey through war and captivity.

A story that embodies brotherhood, humanity, family love, reunions, and separations.

There is no doubt that the Indian government treated, civilian prisoners of war, with dignity and care, and the Pakistani government of that era helped us rebuild our lives.

Yet, many were not as fortunate as us. To this day, some remain trapped in camps in Bangladesh camps that have grown into whole settlements.

Even those who made it to Pakistan had to toil relentlessly to rebuild their lives and provide shelter for their families once more.

Today, when I see chaos and turmoil all around, I sometimes wonder:

Was that captivity better than this so-called freedom? At least in captivity, we found love, humanity, and solidarity.

Now, hatred has overshadowed love. Human life has become cheap. People think only of themselves.

What kind of world awaits future generations? Only time will reveal what story they will write, what pen they will choose to write it with.

****

REVIEWS

Sufyan Khan (He/Him)
Team Lead

MAY 1

Sufyan Khan (He/Him) · 1:22 AM

Dear Khalajan,
As salam o alaikum
I'm Sufyan khan Nawasa of Marhum Naseem Ahmad Khan
I just finished reading your book felt so inspired and proud of.
Your words truly touched my heart and gave me so much to think about.
The way you told your story was both beautifully written and emotional.
It seemed like all this was happening right in front of my eyes.
I have not seen my Nana (he died before my birth).
But people used to talk about his Akhlak,Bravery and commitment Very much.

Now I came to point which compells me to think how unfortuante I'm ?
As I have never seen Marhum Shameem Nana

I could feel your emotions in every lines of chapter.
Your book taught me lessons I'll carry with me always.

Thank you for sharing such a personal and meaningful journey.
I hope more people get to read it and it deserves a wide audience.

Keep me in your Dua, Allah Hafiz

1

Shivangi Singh ★★★★★
04-05-2025

This book isn't just a story, it's a promise, a heartfelt connection between a daughter and her dad. While reading it, I could picture the main character so clearly. He's the focus, but what really stood out to me was the quiet strength behind him, his family. With their love and support, I could see who is narrating the story: his universe "Rose". The book follows his journey from a young boy to a grown man. He holds so much inside, feelings he doesn't always know how to show, but you can tell he wants to. And like the saying goes, "wait for the right time," this book becomes that moment. It's the perfect time for his daughter to keep the promise she made to him. As I read, I noticed how much, as a father, he hid his emotions, the worry in his eyes, the long walks for food, the sleepless nights so his family could rest. But the author saw the weight he carried, and through her pen, she gave it meaning. His journey as a father shaped a woman with a voice, a voice that proves every one of his hardships was worth it. For readers in this Gen Z world, this book can be a reminder of how much our parents do for us, often without saying a word. You'll realize how deep a father's love can go , not through big words, but through the little things they do every day.

Top reviews from India

Avinash Samal

★★★★★ **If you've ever carried pain in your heart, this book will speak to you**

Reviewed in India on 29 April 2025

Reading Dard Ki Lakir felt like sitting quietly with someone who truly understands pain. The author writes with such honesty and softness that you don't feel like you're reading a book—you feel like you're listening to someone's real-life story.

The book doesn't try to impress with big words or dramatic scenes. Instead, it talks about real emotions in a very simple and touching way. Each page made me pause and think, and sometimes even brought tears to my eyes—not because the words were loud, but because they were true.

The author speaks about sadness, silence, and inner strength—especially from the point of view of women and those who often suffer quietly. She just tells it like it is, with respect and depth.

I really appreciated how the book didn't try to give answers or force hope. It just held space for pain, and somehow, that felt healing in itself.

Final Thoughts: Dard Ki Lakir is not just a book—it's an experience. If you've ever carried pain in your heart, this book will speak to you in a way few others can. It's gentle, emotional, and very real.

One person found this helpful

Helpful Report

Rajkumar Prasad

This book by the author title "Dard ki Lakir" depicts the heartache of the country's common people through personal pain in border distribution. May we remember this pain even today and through our experience, to create religious unity on the land of India. If I give my everything, then today the whole country as well as the whole humanity and humanity can be saved from being divided.

Even though the lines were drawn on the ground in the western, the people of India are still maintaining their tradition in maintaining relationships! But at present, the line is being drawn in the hearts of people and the result is in front of us!

From the book "Dard ki Lakir", radical groups should also be informed so that they know how important it is to have peace in India today? If possible, we can all participate in this.

We support the author's effort that, just as he has penned his experience, on the strength of his experience, make a collective and meaningful effort to establish Aman Chan in Hindustan even more beautiful 🙏🙏

Automatically translated

1d Like Reply 1

Arvind Dubey is with **Vishal Verma** and **6 others**.
2d ·

Read 'Dard ki Lakir' written by Mrs. Rozina Khanam ji, wherever you got the opportunity to face different experiences of your personal life closely.
I was introduced to you during my posting (2009-13) as Director of Patna Airport, also got an opportunity to meet your husband Mr. Arshad Khan (Advocate) sir. You gained your distinct identity and popularity while serving Patna especially women through an organization named 'Talent' while busy in social work.
During the partition, I got a lot of information about Hindu people who came from Pakistan to India, but perhaps this was the first opportunity for me when I got first hand information about the migration experience of our Muslim community, any reader. It's natural to get emotional for. The portrayal of historical mistake of humanity's history was heartwarming, especially the writer's words "drawing lines on the ground do not divide relations" resonated in the mind and mind.
I wish for the success of this book giving the message of humanity and humanity.

http://rozinakhanam.co.in/.
site link plus book purchasing link
Line of pain
https://amzn.in/d/2L2jzTp
Rate this translation

Reviews with images

See all photos ›

Top reviews from India

Arshad khan

★★★★★ **Dard ki lakeer**

Reviewed in India on 3 May 2025

Verified Purchase

This powerful and emotional memoir chronicles the author's parents' extraordinary journey through war, civil war, and desperation, showcasing the human spirit's incredible resilience in the face of unimaginable hardship and adversity. The author's writing is exquisite, weaving together the different plot threads with masterful skill, creating a narrative that's both compelling and thought-provoking. The characters are well-developed and relatable, making it easy to become fully invested in their story. I highly recommend 'Dard Ki Lakir' to anyone who loves a good memoir or literary fiction. It's a must-read that showcases the power of storytelling to connect us all, and I have no doubt that it will leave a lasting impact on your heart and mind. 5/5 stars, without a doubt!"

Edit Delete

← **Tagged** Manage

View insights

♡ 363 3

brownboysmoment Book Review: Dard ki Lakir by Rozina Khanam

Genre: Memoir / Historical Non-Fiction
Vibe: Emotional rollercoaster meets history class, but make it personal

Rozina Khanam's Dard ki Lakir isn't just a book—it's a heartfelt time machine packed with emotion, war, survival, and major resilience. It's like opening a family photo album only to find that every picture holds an untold chapter of history. Casual? Not even close. Powerful? 100%.

The book follows the true journey of the author's parents, whose lives took them from India to East Pakistan, through the chaos of civil war and into the heart of Bangladesh's birth. And just when you think things couldn't get heavier, boom—they become prisoners of war in India. But don't worry, it's not all gloom and doom. Rozina threads hope, strength, and a deep sense of love and family through every chapter.

It's not filtered or overly polished—it feels like a late-night chai session with someone's grandma who lived through everything and remembers every detail. You'll walk away knowing a bit more about subcontinental history, yes, but you'll feel it more than anything.

Also, side note: major respect to Rozina's parents—total legends. Imagine living through wars, separation, imprisonment, and still raising a family rooted in love.

TL;DR: If you're into real stories that hit hard, teach you something, and leave you feeling grateful for peace and family, Dard ki Lakir should be at the top of your TBR. It's intimate, intense, and incredibly important. Don't sleep on it. less

14 June

reema.shafi Got a signed copy of 'Dard Ki Lakir'from the author herself Rozina Khanam.

Now Available @ Amazon, Flipkart
Amazon Kindle, Google Play Book.

Some stories stay with you long after you've turned the last page and this is one of them. 'Dard Ki Lakir' is a deeply personal memoir that follows the journey of Rozina's parents from India to East Pakistan, through the heartbreak of war, displacement, and their time as prisoners during the creation of Bangladesh.

But beyond the history, it's the emotions that linger the quiet pain, the deep love, the strength and resilience, especially of women whose voices often go unheard. Rozina writes with such honesty and simplicity, it feels like listening to someone finally share what they've carried silently for years.

If you're drawn to real, lived experiences stories of memory, survival, and quiet courage this book is truly worth reading.

Even more special because it's written by someone we know and love. So proud of you, Rozina khanam 🖤

#DardKiLakir #RozinaKhanam #Memoir #PartitionStories #SubcontinentalHistory #RealStories #WomenInHistory #BookstagramIndia #bluerosepublications less
15 June

← **Tagged** Manage

View insights

19

Liked by **earlymorningmemories** and others

bookswithavinish Book Review

Book:- Line of Pain: From War to Peace
Author:- Rozina Khanam

Eyes have seen a strange scene
Have seen brother imprisoned in brother's house
Those who used to live together like Majaiyo
Today I have seen one Muhafiz and the other imprisoned.

"Line of Pain: From War to Peace" by Rozina Khanam is a touching and lively autobiography that depicts an important journey of South Asia's political and social history through personal experiences. This book is not just the story of a family, but the entire subcontinent that has undergone the complexities of division, war and patriotism.

In this book, the author presents the extraordinary life journey of her parents with truth and sensitivity. The story begins with India, from where their family reached East Pakistan. There they faced political tension, war and ultimately the civil war of 1971, which resulted in the birth of Bangladesh.

After this, their family came to India as a prisoner, where they suffered the difficulties of a prisoned life. Finally they returned to western pakistan (current pakistan). This whole journey was not only geographical, but also extremely challenging emotionally and mentally.

This book provides an opportunity to see big historical events through the eyes of an ordinary family. This perspective is rare, because the experiences of common citizens in most historical writings do not get that much space.

The author's parents story has an amazing glimpse of courage, tolerance and loyalty to her values. Particularly the role of the author's mother presents an empowering image of feminine power in times of struggle.

This book is not just a narrative of pain, but it is also a testament to how even in odd circumstances the human soul does not break, but emerge stronger.

Rozina Khanam's writing style is clear, simple and effective. They have maintained a balance between facts and emotions. There is intimacy in language, which the readers start to feel themselves part of the story.

CONTINUED IN COMMENTS SECTION⬇️⬇️ less

7 hours ago • See original